Peter Neates remarkable 130in. span Handley Page Hannibal is powered by four O.S. FS-60s.

Four-Stroke
Model Engines

Four-Stroke Model Engines

by Peter Miller

Published 1985 by
Traplet Publications Ltd.,
London House,
247-249 Worcester Road,
Malvern Link, Worcestershire WR14 1SY

ISBN 0-9510589-0-8

Cover design by:
Design Action Ltd.

Typeset by Juno Enterprises, Malvern.
Printed in England by:
Billings Books

Acknowledgements

This book could not have been completed without the assistance of a number of people who provided information and engines for test flying and photos. Most photos are by the author except where noted. The Acknowledgements are in alphabetical order of individuals' names with their company in brackets where applicable. To these people and companies, my grateful thanks.

Mike Callaghan (Irvine Engines)
Condor Engines
Bill Cooksey
John D. Haytree (Fox Manufacturing (U.K.) Ltd)
Dick Hill (Ripmax)
F. Kavan
E. E. Lohmolder (Technopower)
MacGregor Ltd
Tony Stephenson (Traplet Publications Ltd)
Neil Tidey (Laser Engines)
Jack Williams
Wik Model

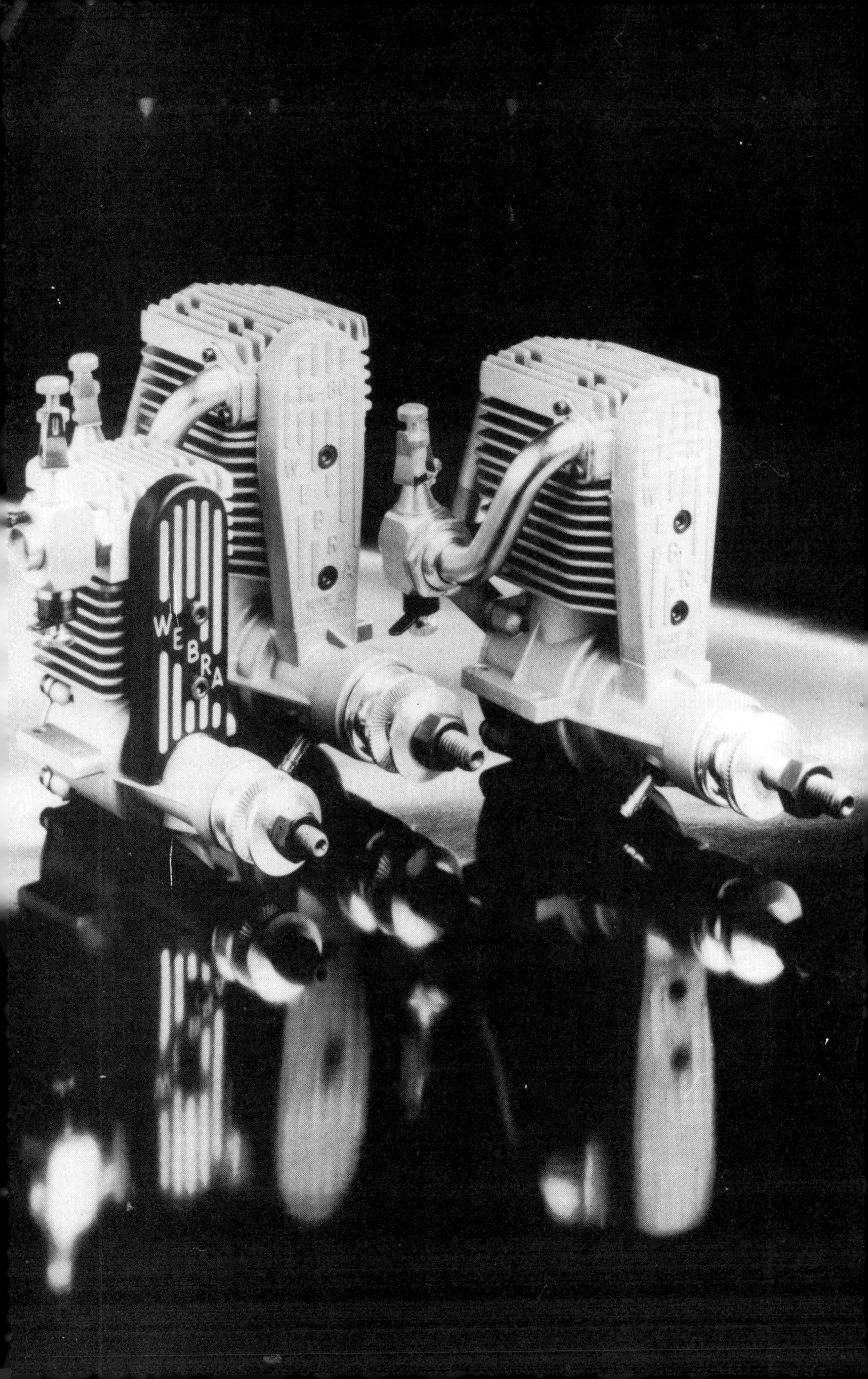
WEBRA

CONTENTS

Webra's three four-strokes, from left to right, the T4-40, T4-80 and T4-60. These are rotary valve engines with the drive belt runing below the cover on the front of the cylinder.

Dedication

This book is dedicated to my mother, Felicity Miller, who, for the last 30 years, has put up with balsa shavings tramped over the house, the smell of dope and glues through the house, mountains of magazines and books scattered around, decorating and household repairs being left for months and even years and a totally neglected garden. Not only has she never complained, she has been totally supporting in all my modelling activities. Without her complete understanding I would never have managed to achieve a tenth of the output that I have. Thanks.

The Morton M-5. This American engine of the 1940s is a valuable collectors engine. — Bill Cooksey photo.

Introduction

Four-stroke engines are relatively new to the modelling scene but their popularity has been quite amazing. The author soon became totally addicted to them for a number of reasons and has flown all the smaller ones up to .60 cu.in. plus a few of the larger ones.

Two-stroke engines have a number of books devoted to their operation and use, but after talking to other modellers and reading various magazines, it became obvious that there was a need for a book devoted to the four-stroke. This book is the result.

Because of the fairly recent advent of the four-stroke and the rapid increase in power and types by different manufacturers, no claim can be made that this book is definitive. However, it does cover all engines made up to the time of writing and the principles of operation and application will continue to be valid, regardless of future developments. Hopefully it will help modellers get the best out of their engines and save them from expensive mistakes.

The chapter on flight test reports is unique and can be used to decide what model would suit a particular engine or what engine will best suit the modeller's preferred type of model.

Four-strokes are a joy to use and enjoyment is the whole object of aeromodelling. If this book helps a few more modellers to get a little more pleasure out of their hobby it will have succeeded in its purpose.

The Kalt 45, first of the modern four-strokes.

The O.S. FS-60, the engine that really started the four-stroke explosion in this country. — Tony Stephenson photos.

Chapter 1

The Third Revolution

The story of model aircraft engine development has been one of steady progress over the years. This progress has been marked by two dramatic events which instantly changed the whole picture. In Europe the development of the compression ignition engine virtually eliminated the spark ignition engine, while in the United States of America the glowplug had the same effect. This division of types remained for several years, each side of the Atlantic trying the other system with varying degrees of success, although in general the glowplug achieved greater acceptance in Europe than the diesel did in the USA. Gradually the glowplug took over in Europe until it was the most common form of engine in use.

The third great change in engine design is the four-stroke. While this change was not as rapid as the two previous ones it has taken place throughout the world and is still expanding. Four-strokes are not new, of course, model engineers have been building them for as long as the full size engines have existed and they have been used to power model aircraft for the same length of time. However, these were one-offs and production engines were few and far between. The Feeny 4-cycle was made in the USA and this is a very rare engine today. The first really mass produced four-stroke was originally financed by the United States Air Force. This was the famous Morton M-5, later known as the Burgess and it was intended to be used as a training aid for Air Force mechanics. A five-cylinder overhead-valve radial engine, it was not very powerful and needed constant attention to keep it running.

In Britain there were two engines made for the boating fraternity, the Gannet and the Channel Island Special, which very occasionally were

The Technopower 7 in Lloyd Ressler's PT 17, a beautiful four-stroke in a beautiful model.

adapted for use in model aircraft. A few years ago the engines now made in the USA under the name Technopower were developed in Ireland. In all these cases the price put the engines out of reach of the average modeller. Then O.S. introduced the FS-60 and Kalt brought out the Kalt 45 at prices comparable to the more expensive two-strokes. These engines were very quiet, very economical on fuel and sounded perfect in scale models, they also offered a new experience in model flying. They were not particularly powerful and initially most were probably bought for the novelty but soon modellers realised that they were useful power plants and the flood began. Other engines appeared, more power was extracted and bigger and bigger engines were built, the third revolution had arrived. The four-stroke has now become so popular that international contest rules have been changed to allow four-strokes of up to 20cc capacity to be used while still retaining the maximum of 10ccs for two-strokes. The original proposals allowed for four-strokes up to 15cc but this was increased to the present limit before the rule became effective. It will be interesting to see the end result of this rule change because the constant improvements in power output will soon mean that four-strokes will equal two-strokes. This has already happened in one or two cases, the British Laser 61 being a good example.

The four-stroke is ideally suited to a number of applications. Vintage modellers find that it is a perfect match for the R/C assist vintage model. At a Vintage rally in 1984, R/C assist models powered by four-strokes out-numbered those powered by all other types of engine and the standard two-stroke was the least popular of all.

The four-stroke is extremely useful for scale models where the sound combined with large propellers gives a far greater degree of realism, provided that the right subject is chosen. For example, a Pitts Special does not sound right with the four-stroke as the original has a much harsher engine note, the model needs to give an impression of tremendous power to look and sound realistic. On the other hand a Tiger Moth is perfect with a four-stroke and one incident can illustrate this. A model Tiger Moth, built from the Pilot kit and powered by an Enya 35-4C, was being flown from a strip where a full size Tiger was based. People at the next farm later mentioned to the full size Tiger owner that he had been seen flying on that Sunday, when in fact the full size Tiger was in the hangar with the tailplane removed.

The introduction of the FAI "turn-around" pattern for aerobatic contests has led many aerobatic modellers to investigate the larger four-strokes, because the schedule must be flown in a limited space which calls for slower models. At the time of writing no definite conclusions have been reached although results seem promising.

Away from the contest scene the ordinary sports flier is finding that

Enya 60-4C, this is the marine version. Model four-strokes have been used in boats for many years, the boating fraternity are now benefitting from the popularity of four-strokes for model aircraft. — Ripmax photo.

Saito FA 40 cylinder head showing hemispherical combustion chamber. This engine has had several hours running and yet there is virtually no carbon build up.

the four-stroke is an ideal powerplant due to its quietness and fuel economy and a large number of plans and kits designed with the four-stroke as the preferred engine are becoming available.

The question now must be, why have four-strokes become so popular when they seem to have several points against them? They are much more complex than the two-stroke, they are more vulnerable to crash damage, they are more expensive than comparable two-strokes and they do not have as much specific power output. Other types of engine suffering from these disadvantages have either fallen by the wayside, for example the Aero 35 which featured the cylinder lying parallel to the crankshaft, or they have only continued to be made in one size by one manufacturer as has the O.S. Wankel engine. Possibly the fact that these two engines departed from the conventional layout that modellers are used to was a major factor in their lack of general acceptance while the four-stroke not only resembles the ordinary two-stroke in appearance but most modellers are used to the idea of the four-stroke concept from their own car or motorcycle and so a psychological barrier is avoided.

The four-stroke does have a number of advantages over the two-stroke. It is much quieter, in most cases it is quieter without a silencer than an equivalent two-stroke fitted with a good silencer, and when the four-stroke is fitted with a silencer it becomes extremely quiet. Add to this the fact that a four-stroke silencer is a much smaller and neater device than the usual big sausage fitted to two strokes, with consequent problems in cowling the engine and untidy appearance, and you have an immediate practical and aesthetic advantage.

The four-stroke is very economical on fuel, some engines use less than a third of the amount of fuel per flying hour than a two-stroke of the same size. This particular advantage is being slowly reduced as fuel consumption rises due to the increased power being developed by the newer engines. Some engines prefer fuels with a high Nitromethane content while a few need no Nitromethane at all. The lower fuel consumption offsets the added expense of high Nitromethane content to a degree.

The four-stroke will swing bigger diameter propellers, at lower r.p.m., than the two-stroke, this is a major advantage because it is more efficient to move a lot of air slowly than to move a small amount fast. This means that it is often possible that a large model will fly better with a four-stroke turning a large propeller than it will with an engine of higher nominal power which has to use a small propeller to reach its optimum power range. The larger propeller is also useful when a scale model has a large radial cowled engine.

Turning to the less practical but none the less important points in favour of the four-stroke. These engines have a character of their own

Dr Jeremy Shaw's 15 ft. span, 72 lb Grumman Albatross is powered by two three cylinder Magnum engines of 45cc capacity each and is equipped with on board starters.

The combustion chamber in the head of the Webra .40 4-T showing the rotary valve port. Glowplug fits in the side of the head.

which words cannot describe but which must be experienced to be appreciated. There can be no doubt that there is considerable pleasure to be had in owning and operating a complex piece of precision machinery which is reliable and useful. This factor probably strongly supports the popularity of the four-stroke. Few modellers who have seen them in operation have failed to be impressed and most promptly get a strong desire to own one themselves.

There is one other area which the four-stroke has helped considerably and this is the field of multi-cylinder engines. Twin cylinder, and even four, five and six cylinder engines, have been available for many years. However, the two-stroke twin has always suffered from the problem of uneven charging of the cylinders and this has been compounded in the four and six cylinder engines which may be considered as multiples of twins. To a large extent these problems have been overcome by the remarkable engines made by G-Mark, but they have not been completely eliminated. Radial two-stroke engines have had to have five separate engines geared together and all these engines have suffered from frictional losses, which is a serious factor in a two-stroke which needs to run at high r.p.m. to obtain the best power output. The four-stroke has overcome all these problems and twin cylinder engines are comparatively common, while flat fours and sixes are available from O.S. Three, five, seven and nine cylinder radial engines are available from Technopower, while O.S. have a five cylinder radial coming out and Saito has a flat twin available. At the time of writing the CAP .60 cu.in. in-line twin has only just become available. Magnum make a "V" twin and three cylinder radial, Laser have a "V" twin and Knights of the Air in the USA is planning a limited run of a ⅕th scale fourteen cylinder twin row Pratt & Whitney Wasp of around 240ccs capacity.

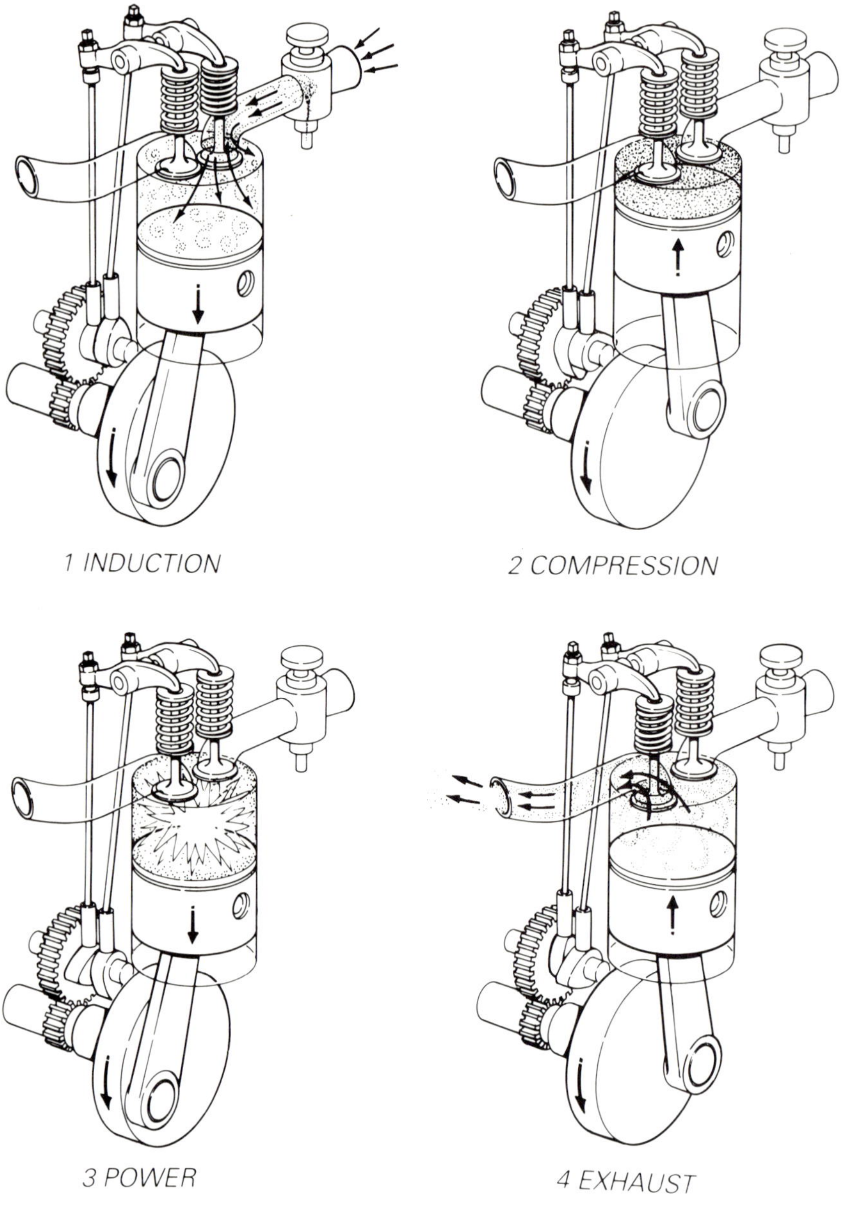

FOUR-STROKE CYCLE

Chapter 2

Principles and Variations

The main mechanical difference between a two-stroke and four-stroke is that, as the names imply, the complete cycle of operation in a two-stroke takes place in one upward and one downward stroke of the piston, while the four-stroke uses two upward and two downward strokes of the piston. The two-stroke fires the fuel mixture once every revolution of the crankshaft and the four-stroke once every two revolutions.

The complete cycle of operation of a two-stroke is simple to describe. The piston moves up creating a reduction of pressure in the crankcase which sucks in the fuel/air mixture while at the same time compressing the previous mixture charge in the cylinder. When the piston reaches the top of its upward stroke the compressed mixture ignites and the rapid expansion of gasses forces the piston down, the action also compresses the mixture in the crankcase. Towards the bottom of the downward stroke the piston uncovers first the exhaust port, which allows the burnt gasses to escape, then further downward movement uncovers the transfer port which allows the gasses in the crankcase to pass into the cylinder and the whole cycle starts again.

The operation of the four-stroke is more complex. The piston starting at the top of the cylinder moves downwards with the inlet valve open, this sucks in the fuel/air mixture and is called the induction stroke. With both valves closed the piston travels back up the cylinder compressing the mixture, this is the compression stroke. At about the top of the stroke the mixture ignites forcing the piston back down, this is the power stroke. When the piston starts back up the cylinder the exhaust valve opens allowing the burnt gasses to be pushed out of the cylinder on what is called the exhaust stroke.

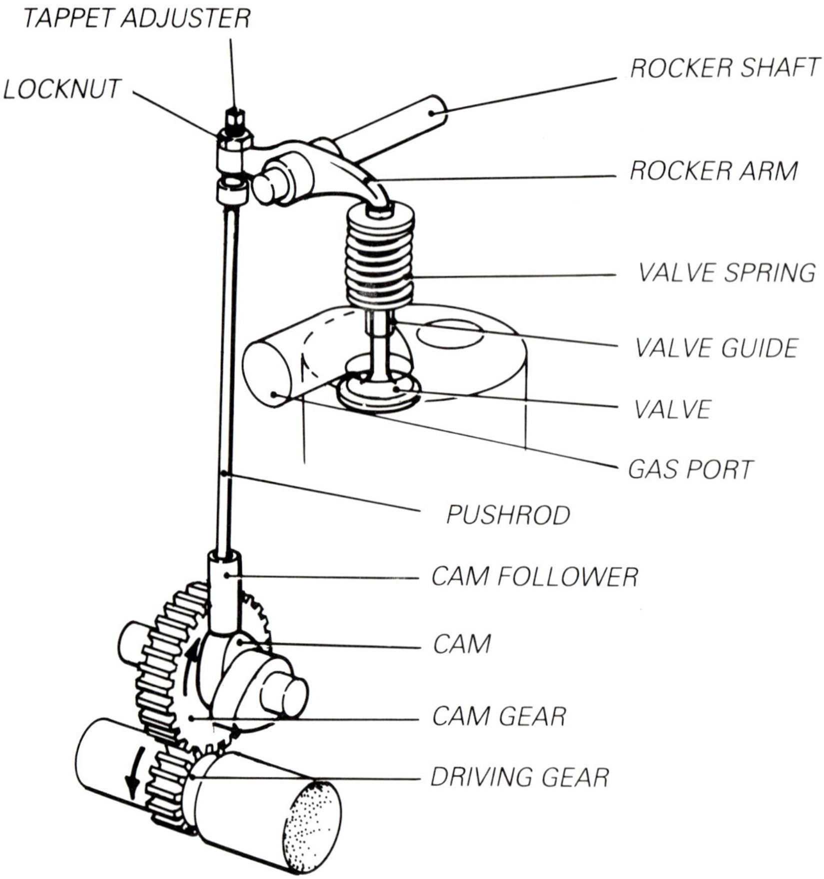
TAPPET ADJUSTER
LOCKNUT
ROCKER SHAFT
ROCKER ARM
VALVE SPRING
VALVE GUIDE
VALVE
GAS PORT
PUSHROD
CAM FOLLOWER
CAM
CAM GEAR
DRIVING GEAR

From the descriptions it will be seen that the two-stroke has one power stroke for every revolution of the crankshaft while the four-stroke only has one power stroke every two crankshaft revolutions and this would seem to indicate that the two-stroke should be more powerful by the ratio of 2:1 but this is not so. The fact that the piston of the two-stroke opens the exhaust port before it reaches the bottom of its stroke means that some of the force of the gasses are wasted, also because of the need to flush out all the exhaust gasses, some of the fresh charge of gas escapes through the still open exhaust port, so it can be seen that the two-stroke cannot use the fuel as efficiently as the four-stroke. The four-stroke uses the full length of the induction stroke to draw in fuel, the full length of the compression stroke to compress it and the full power stroke to extract the maximum useful energy from the burning gasses and finally, the exhaust stroke clears almost every bit of burnt gas from the cylinder.

The four-stroke does have or two items working against it which must be offset against the efficiency with which it uses its fuel. The gas passages are much smaller than those on a two-stroke which can reduce the amount of gas sucked in and increase the work done by the piston on the exhaust stroke and the engine not only has to move the crankshaft, piston and propeller as does the two-stroke, it also has to power the valve mechanism which can absorb some of the power produced.

The four-stroke relies on valves in the cylinder head to control the flow of gasses. These valves are of two basic types, the poppet valve and the rotary valve and do the same job in completely different ways.

The poppet valve is a mushroom shaped component which is held against its seat by spring pressure. A camshaft is driven by the crankshaft at half crankshaft speed and these cams operate pushrods which in turn operate levers on the cylinder head called rocker arms. The opposite end of the rocker arm presses down on the valve to open it and then as the cam continues to turn removing the operating pressure from the pushrod and rocker arm the valve spring closes the valve.

The rotary valve can take three forms, all driven at half the crankshaft speed either by gears and shafts or by toothed belts. The valve may be a vertical cylinder in the head, it may be a horizontal cylinder or it may take the form of a disc. Each type has holes or ports which uncover the inlet and exhaust port in turn as the valve rotates. In some engines the rotary valve also covers and uncovers the glowplug as well, which helps to prevent the glowplug from being cooled down by the incoming mixture, an advantage for slow running or if the engine is running with a very rich mixture i.e. a higher than normal amount of fuel in the fuel/air mixture!

Both the poppet and rotary valves have their advantages and disad-

The exposed portions of the valve mechanism on an early Saito 40, later versions have enclosed pushrods and rocker arms. Note tappet adjuster at front of rocker arm, feeler gauge goes between valve stem and rocker arm (left side of photo).

vantages. The poppet valve is easier to seal, in most cases has less friction, can be adjusted to take up any wear in the system and will normally allow a more efficient shape in the combustion chamber. Against it is the large number of parts that go into the valve train, the smaller gas ports inherent in the design and the limitations on high r.p.m. This last is caused by the fact that the many reciprocating parts cannot react fast enough and the valve can "float" and even hit the piston in extreme cases. It should be stressed that with any current engine one would have to use a very small propeller to reach these limits.

The rotary valve has a much lower parts count, can employ larger gas ports and does not suffer from valve float, it is less liable to crash damage and wear should not be a problem because the loads on the bearing surfaces are quite light. Against the rotary valve is the fact that it is harder to get the optimum shape for the combustion chamber and greater precision is needed in manufacture to get a good, long lasting, gas tight seal. The German manufacturers tend to favour the rotary valve, the Japanese favour the poppet valve while British manufacturers use both but with the poppet valve ahead of the rotary valve. From the owner's point of view there seems to be little difference in actual operation of the engine so the type of valve should not be a major factor in the choice of an engine.

Looking at the different poppet valve engines two things will be noticed, they are all over head valve engines (o.h.v.) and that the camshafts are located in a variety of places. The Saito range use a camshaft driven by spur gears and lying above and parallel with the crankshaft, the O.S. engines have the camshaft above and across the crankshaft driven by skew gears or at the rear of the engine driven by spur gears, the Enya engines use two separate camshafts mounted at the rear and driven by spur gears and the Laser 61 uses the same method as does the Magnum. They all work well and the only point worth mentioning is that the rear mounted camshaft types will be slightly less vulnerable to crash damage.

The carburettors used on four-strokes are exactly the same types as those used on two-strokes except that they look very small when compared with that on a two-stroke of the same size. Some of the newer carbs feature chokes of various designs, which is a very useful feature, and on many engines the carb is mounted on a manifold pipe so that the carb is nearer to the usual level on a two-stroke, this is so that fuel tank location will not have to be changed in a model. Not all engines have been tested and found to have sufficient fuel draw not to be affected by the tank/carb relationship.

The lubrication of a two-stroke is by means of oil carried in the fuel, as the fuel mixture is passed through the crankcase some of the oil is de-

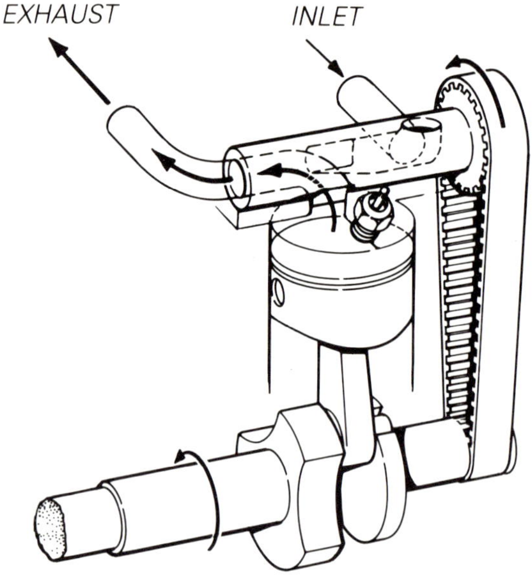

CROSS ROTARY VALVE

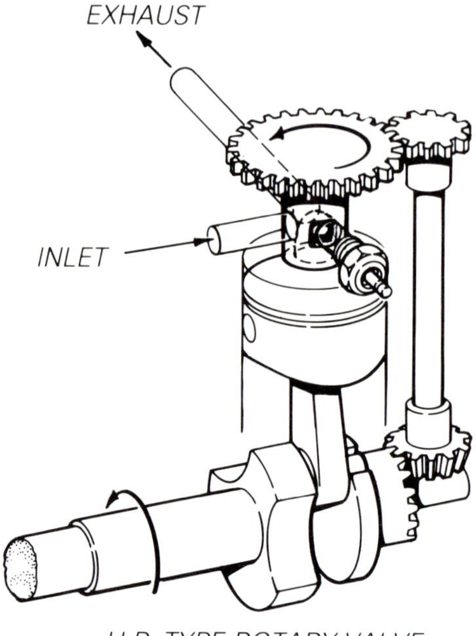

H.P. TYPE ROTARY VALVE

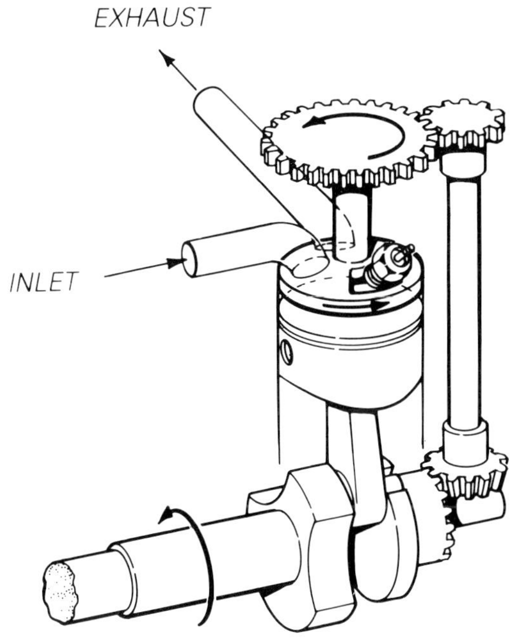

DISC ROTARY VALVE

posited on the various surfaces while the positive pressure in the crankcase that forces the mixture into the cylinder also forces some of the oil along the crankshaft to lubricate the bearings.

The lubrication of a four-stroke also depends on oil carried in the fuel. However, apart from one or two engines, the fuel mixture does not pass through the crankcase and so lubrication of the lower parts of the engine relies on oil being forced past the piston. This system may seem rather inefficient but one only has to see the amount of oil that is ejected from the crankcase breather tube and front bearing to see that there is adequate lubrication and in fact special fuels for four-strokes have a much lower oil content that that used for normal two-strokes.

The HP VT engines do use a more positive method of lubrication, they take a pipe from the silencer to the valve gears in the cylinder head which carries some of the unburnt oil from the exhaust and, using the pressure from the exhaust force the oil down past the gear shaft into the crankcase where it is pushed along the crank shaft housing to a second pipe connection. This pipe is led back to the fuel tank with the result that the fuel is slightly pressurised to help with the fuel feed to the carb and

HP VT 21 rotary valve, this engine has the valve vertical in the head. The valve is the combustion chamber in this engine.

The uinique vane pump on the Saito FA 90T flat twin, this pump pressurises the crankcase to prevent blow-by of corrosive fumes past the piston and to flush away any that do get past via the breather nipple fitted in the crankshaft housing.

the oil that would normally be pumped to atmosphere is fed to the tank instead. While this does ensure really good lubrication it does have the disadvantage that the corrosive exhaust gasses are deliberately fed through the engine and that any metal particles picked up in the engine will eventually be carried through the engine again with the fuel. A good filter in the fuel line should reduce any risk of damage from this source.

The few engines that do pass the fresh gas charge through the crankcase will be less likely to suffer from corrosion. The Saito twins have a special pump fitted to pressurise the crankcase, this is incorporated because, due to the layout of the engine the crankcase volume does not change in the same way that it does on single cylinder engines or twins which have the pistons moving in or out together. The Saito has only one crankpin and so as one piston moves out the opposite one moves inwards. Ways to prevent corrosion will be described in the chapter on car and maintenance.

This front view of the O.S. FS 40 (left) and Saito FA-40 shows the two approaches to the front camshaft layout. O.S. engine has a non standard extension to the needle valve, Saito provide a proper extension which has not been fitted here.

The 50cc Kavan is a replica of the front two cylinders of the full size Continental engine. It is unusual in that it has a wet sump with oil pump for lubrication.

Chapter 3

Choosing a Four Stroke

All the current production engines are good reliable power units, but there is a great variety of types and sizes and, just as some two-strokes are better suited for one type of model, so it is with four-strokes. Of course they can all be used with most types of model but if a modeller is mainly interested in one general class it makes sense to buy the engine most suited to that class or at least, most suited to the first model that he plans to put the engine in.

The four-stroke is no harder to operate than a two-stroke and can be easier in many cases, however the novice is recommended not to buy a four-stroke as his first engine for the simple reason that they do need a little more maintenance and they are much more vunerable to the inevitable crashes that the beginner will suffer. Having said that, it is well known that many people starting in the hobby decide what they want regardless of its suitability, (any model shop proprietor can tell tales of the raw recruit insisting on starting with a Spitfire) so if it is a four-stroke or nothing the beginner should choose an engine with fully enclosed valves and the carburettor at the rear, or at least one of the rotary valve engines which is unlikely to suffer more damage than the average two-stroke.

The experienced modeller will have a better idea of what he wants from the engine, even so, there are a number of factors to be taken into account. These will depend on the type of model in which the engine will mainly be used, scale, vintage, sports aerobatic or fully aerobatic.

Taking the scale modeller first. The person who likes short nosed aircraft with radial cowls such as the Camel would do well to choose a heavy engine with the carb in front of the engine. The HP VT49 springs to mind as it weighs 20½ ounces and fits the other requirements as well. The Saito range are excellent for blending into an exposed dummy radial engine while the Enya range tend to be more compact and will fit inside cowlings such as the Tiger Moth, they will also make a reasonable match for one side of a Volkswagon engine. The O.S. range will also suit this type of model. It is not a good idea to mount an engine with exposed rockers etc, in the inverted position so if that type of aircraft is the most popular there is an obvious point to avoid.

The Vintage enthusiast will find that any of the four-strokes are excellent for his purpose. The slight, or sometimes considerable, extra weight is an advantage on the short nosed designs of the past. The power output of the four-stroke is much nearer to that of vintage engines which used relatively large propellers at low r.p.m. Most Vintage models are light or have a low wing loading and so do not need over large engines. A first generation O.S. FS-60 will fly a Keil Kraft Falcon quite happily and that is an 8ft span model with fairly heavy construction. The Saito 30 will fly a 63in. span Junior 60 at half throttle and will even aerobat a 5lb Super 60. The vintage modeller is in the lucky position of merely having to decide on the size of engine and the price he wants to pay with any other considerations being based on personal preferance.

The sports flier is in a similar position to the vintage modeller. However, if he plans to use the engine in a range of commercially available kits or plans it might be a good idea to look at the lighter engines to avoid having to add too much weight in the tail, and as some designs do not allow for the extra length of some four-strokes, the engines with front valve gear would be advisable. Remember, if you just lengthen the bearers you will be adding to the problem of a heavy engine, the best answer here is to move the firewall back if possible.

The use of four-strokes for aerobatics is still under investigation by many of the top pilots and this, combined with the new turn around pattern, means that the whole subject is open to different approaches before any definite formula can be laid down.

The four-stroke is proving to be an excellent engine for endurance records due to its remarkable fuel economy. The engines used for this purpose are usually converted to spark ignition which improves even further in the area of economy. This is now such a specialised area that the average modeller is unlikely to attempt a world record but national records might be worth considering and here one would choose one of the less powerful engines because more power uses more fuel, regardless of throttle setting.

Racing is one area where the four-stroke has no place, but the increasing speeds and technology required are taking racing out of reach of most modellers. Even Club 20 seems to be creeping into the realms of specialisation so perhaps a special class for four-strokes would be popular, it would certainly be quieter.

Considering the extra complexity of the four-stroke they are very reasonably priced. Some are cheaper than a high performance two-stroke of the same capacity, but they are still quite an expensive item to many modellers and so there may be a temptation to buy a second hand engine. This can be much cheaper, it could also be much more expensive.

Buying a used two-stroke is basically safe and simple as one can easily check such vital items as compression and wear but a four-stroke is not such a simple task. The compression can be tested easily enough and poor compression may be caused by a leaking valve, on the other hand it may be much more serious. A new cylinder head with valves would be very expensive to replace.

The biggest problem with a used four-stroke is the possiblity of corrosion. If the previous owner has not taken care of the engine the bearings could well be in a poor state, the cams and gears may be corroded and any bits of corrosion breaking off will soon wear out the rest of the engine. For this reason it would be best to buy a used engine from a good model shop or from a fellow club member so that in the event of any failure the engine could be returned or the cost of repairs refunded.

If the engine is being bought from someone not known to you, it is best to make sure that the engine is in good condition and several checks can be made. The compression can be tested by turning the engine over, the plug should then be removed and the engine turned over very slowly, there should be slight resistance as the cams lift the valves but there should be no feeling of roughness. On most engines it is possible to remove either the front housing or the backplate without too much trouble and it is worth insisting on doing this and finally the engine should be run. While it is running look at the colour of the oil coming from the breather nipple, it should be almost clear, also look for brown coloured oil seeping from the front bearing, a sure sign of corrosion on the crankshaft and bearings.

All this may seem a bit alarmist but bear in mind that the repair bill could quite easily be twice the saving made by buying a used engine. Not all owners are careful about protecting their engines and there are a number of engines around that were in use before the problem of corrosion was discovered.

The first four-stroke designed for car use in the HP VT-21 car. It is distinguished by a heat sink head and slide carburettor.

Chapter 4

Operation of the Four Stroke

The four-stroke engine is, as has been said, far more complex than a two-stroke but the added complexity does not mean that it is harder to operate. They are not and in some ways are easier to start, but handling techniques are slightly different.

The new owner of a four-stroke is strongly advised to mount the engine on a test stand and get used to starting it and setting it before installing it in a model. This time can also be usefully spent in doing the initial running in of the engine.

Before starting the new engine read the instructions carefully, then read them again and make sure that they have been understood, that the correct size of propeller is fitted and that the correct fuel is being used. Where a range of props is given but no recommendation for running in is mentioned use one of the smaller sizes with a fine pitch so as not to load the engine too much. Once everything is set up comes the great moment.

Four-strokes like to be "wet" for starting. If a choke is fitted use it in accordance with the instructions, if not, finger choke the engine until the carb is wet, some engines will not suck neat fuel up from the carb and here, a few drops of fuel down the exhaust pipe is a good idea. Now turn the engine over to make sure that there is not so much fuel in the cylinder that the engine will not turn over, a hydraulic lock can wreck an engine. Next give the engine a couple of flicks and connect the battery to the glowplug and flick the engine over, it is quite likely that the engine will start at once although sometimes several flicks are needed.

Sometimes an engine will kick back as it is flicked, this may be due to excess fuel and the proper thing to do is to bring the prop round slowly anti-clockwise until compression is felt and then flick it backwards. The prop will go through about one and a half revolutions, come up to compression and fire, this will often start the engine and will certainly clear any excess fuel, the technique is known as the backwards flick or "bounce flick" start. With this method the prop is not flicked through compression.

A word of warning now, quite often an engine that is wet will start and eject a large amount of raw fuel through the exhaust pipe, if this is pointing upwards an assistant standing behind the engine will get a faceful of fuel so either point the exhaust pipe in a safe direction or warn your helper.

The author prefers starting his engines on full throttle, but it is safer to start them on half throttle especially when mounted in a model, as there is less risk of the model running forward and causing injury. Follow the instructions on this point until you are familiar with the engine.

Once the engine starts make sure that it is running rich, this is shown by plenty of smoke and oil coming from the exhaust pipe. If the engine has been started with the throttle partly closed open it at once on the first few runs, this is because the intermediate fuel mixture is not always controlled by the high speed needle valve and so the engine may not be rich enough at reduced throttle. The rich setting is to ensure plenty of lubrication and it also keeps the engine cooler.

The engine will need running in or, as some instructions call it, breaking in. This is particularly important with four-strokes as there are far more moving parts and the valves are moving in the cylinder head which is the hottest part of the engine. If the engine is run with too lean a setting at this stage there is a risk of damaging it. The instructions in many cases say that the engine can be run in the air. However, the author prefers to run at least two tankfulls of fuel through the engine on the ground, the first very rich, so rich that the engine will only just keep running with the plug disconnected, and the second slightly leaner, a total of about half an hours running. This has several advantages, if anything is going to fail it will often do so in the very early stages, this has only happened once in several hundred hours with a large number of engines so is not a serious risk, the second thing is that if the engine starts to lean out as the fuel level drops the needle valve can be opened at once. Fortunately most four-strokes are quiet enough to be run in the garden for short periods although it is not recommended. It is strange but true that some neighbours will object even though they can't hear the engine over the sound of their lawnmower.

Running in in the air does allow the model to be flown sooner than would otherwise be the case. The engine should be set on the rich side and long climbs at full throttle should be avoided. The best method is to spend some time on each flight flying Cuban Eights, assuming the pilot is capable of these, or, if not, an experienced pilot should be asked to do them. The reason for the Cuban Eights is that it alternatively applies some load to the engine followed by a very lightly loaded period so that it can cool down. Over the first few flights the needle valve can be closed to lean the engine out until the engine will hold full r.p.m. without any sign of sagging or tightening up. If at any stage it does show such signs land at once and richen the mixture again.

Setting the needle on a fully run in engine is quite simple. Screw it in until the engine just starts to slow down after reaching max r.p.m. As soon as this stage is reached open the needle and again the engine will pick up speed. Continue to open the needle slowly until the first hint of r.p.m. drop and that is the safe setting. Should the engine show signs of loosing power when the model is held nose up, open the needle a click more at a time until the model can be held nose up without losing r.p.m.

After the first hour of running check the valve clearances and re-set them if necessary. It is quite likely that they will need re-setting at this stage. More will be said about this in the chapter on care and maintenance.

The different engines have varying fuel requirements, the Laser range for example do not need any nitromethane and straight Castor/methanol fuel is the only one to use with these engines, while the Enya range recommend up to 15% Nitromethane but may need an extra cylinder head shim fitting. This is provided with the 40-4C and 46-4C. The Enya 35-4C did not provide this and in fact is better on low nitro fuels. The 35-4C is no longer listed but there are still some around. This engine may be run on straight fuel with large propellers.

The running in of an engine should always be carried out with a normal two-stroke glow fuel. Such a fuel contains at least 20% oil. Once the engine has been run in it may be run on four-stroke fuel which contains 10% oil. This will give more power, a better and more reliable idle and a cleaner model but when using a fuel with low oil content one must be extremely careful to avoid leaning the engine out too much. A Castor oil is better than a synthetic oil because it will stand up to the extra heat generated in a lean run and so will give some reserve of protection. Many top racing experts who use synthetic oils add 3% Castor oil for this reason.

There are some engines which do not use a separate needle valve to set the low speed mixture. A few of these engines may hunt i.e. the r.p.m. may rise and fall at fast throttle settings or the needle valve may be difficult to set for optimum running when using four-stroke fuel. This is caused by slight fuel leakages in the carb due to the thinner fuel and the problem will often be cured by reverting to normal two-stroke fuel.

Enya 60-4C. This is one of the more powerful .60 cu.in. engines. — Ripmax photo.

Connector for plugs

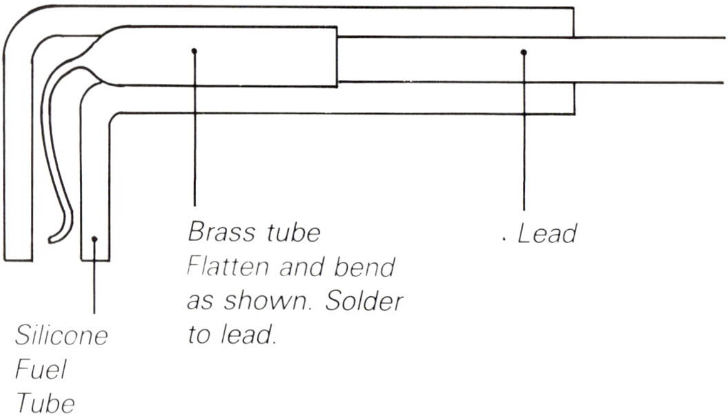

The Swedish Damo flat twin is a most unusual engine in that it is designed to run on pure methanol with no oil at all. This is achieved by using needle roller bearings throughout and very hard surfaces. There is some slight lubrication obtained from the methanol itself but this would not seem to be significant. The Damo is the only engine that has ever specified such a fuel and any attempt to run any other engine this way would result in the engine being totally ruined in a matter of seconds.

Most current four-strokes provide a pressure tap in the exhaust system which is used to pressurise the fuel tank. This slight pressurisation will provide a very reliable fuel flow and should be used. The HP VT engines use a system where this pressure is fed from the silencer to the valve gears in the cylinder head, down to the crankcase, through the front bearing and out of a nipple in the front housing and then back to the tank. This does keep the model cleaner and ensures good lubrication of the gears but as any small particles from the engine may be carried back to the tank and then back through the engine a filter should be fitted to the fuel line. This filter should be examined regularly to prevent it becoming clogged (see VT 21 flight test).

Some engines do not have any provision for taking pressure from the exhaust. Here the manufacturer will have carried out extensive tests and will have found that it is not important on that particular engine. If one feels that, for some reason, pressure is needed, perhaps because the tank has to be a long way from the engine, it may be possible to fit a pressure adaptor from another make of engine such as an O.S. Never connect the crankcase breather to the tank, it could cause a build up of oil in the crankcase and will waste power because the engine will have to work against the pressure in the crankcase that is now unable to escape, also the pressures will probably be high enough to make setting the needle valve very critical. Note that the HP engines are open to the exhaust system so there is no build up of pressure and that two strokes that use crankcase pressure are racing engines and that the crankcase is open to atmosphere for part of the cycle.

Some engines are fitted with glowplugs from the factory while quite a few manufacturers do not supply a plug. All the instructions recommend certain plugs for that particular engine, but some types or makes may not be available from your local model shop. The huge range of makes and types makes it impractical for any but the largest shops to carry such a stock.

The four-stroke does not need a plug with an idle bar but it does need a "hot" plug, that is one that will keep glowing over the complete cycle of the engine. Some engines, notably the Laser 61, are completely non-critical on plugs and it has been found that most four-strokes are quite happy on a wide range of plugs with no noticeable loss of power.

There are two good indications of an unsuitable plug having been fitted. Assuming that the carb is correctly set for both fast and low speed and the plug is new, if there is an audible drop in r.p.m. when the battery is disconnected, or if the engine will not idle reliably, the plug is too "cold" and a hotter plug should be fitted. The author has found that Taylor plus and Fox 1½ volt plugs give very good results but stresses that this is a personal choice and that other plugs will be just as good. O.S. and Enya make special four-stroke plugs which are, as would be expected, extremely good but are more expensive.

If one is searching for maximum power one should get hold of a tachometer and test a range of different plugs on a particular engine. However, unless the plug is completely unsuitable the gain in r.p.m. is unlikely to be more than 100–200 r.p.m. and this is not enough to concern the average four-stroke owner.

The propeller is one factor that will make a tremendous difference to the power output of the engine. An engine that seems to lack power on one propeller will be transformed by changing to another type or size and it is very important to match the propeller not only to the engine but to the aircraft as well.

Plain nylon propellers should not be used. As the power of the engine increases this becomes more important. At the high r.p.m. generated by two-strokes nylon propellers can throw blades with the serious risk of injury to the operator or spectators. The four-stroke will also cause nylon propellers to throw blades but not due to high r.p.m. What happens is that the power stroke of the engine accelerates the prop from the hub but the tips tend to resist this and "lag" behind the hub. The engine then slows over the next three strokes, especially the compression stroke, so that the hub is being slowed by the engine while the tips are carried on by inertia and start to "lead". As soon as the engine fires the whole sequence starts again with the result that there is a constant chordwise flexing of the propeller, which can rapidly lead to fatigue and failure. One modeller had three such failures in succession which brought the problem into the open.

The safest propellers are made from glass filled nylon or wood, these are stiffer and, in the case of wood, lighter which reduces the loading and flexing and therefore the fatigue.

Flight testing a large number of models and engines has shown that the four-stroke gives its best performance on a wide bladed propeller in the lower pitch ranges and two examples of this are given. A large model of a Polish homebuilt aircraft fitted with an Enya 40-4C in the pusher configuration was flown on a home made 11¾ x 5in. propeller with wide blades. It flew very well on this prop but power became marginal on any other. The second example was a $\frac{2}{9}$th scale Turbulent. Originally powered by a Saito FA-40 it had a good flight performance, an Enya 46-4C was fitted with a narrow blade propeller and even though the engine was far more powerful, the flight performance was reduced. A Graupner 12 x 5in. wide blade prop was fitted and the performance jumped dramatically. More details of these models will be found in the section on flight tests.

It is possible that a wide bladed propeller may not be available in the size required for a particular engine/model combination. The answer is to buy a larger diameter propeller and cut it down to the required diameter and re-balance it.

It is always important to balance a propeller. This applies just as much to four-strokes as two-strokes. Due to the fact that a four-stroke fires only once every two revolutions and that the r.p.m. is generally lower than the two-stroke, the vibration frequency is lower and of a greater amplitude. There is nothing that can be done about this but if the propeller is out of balance the effects will be far more pronounced and a second vibration frequency may be generated. A properly balanced propeller will eliminate one source of vibration.

When selecting a propeller from the range of sizes given in the engine's instructions, it is worth remembering that it is more efficient to move a large amount of air slowly than a small amount fast, so start testing the engine/model combination with low pitch, large diameter propellers. By all means try propellers at the other end of the range and note how the performance changes. It is only by such experiments that the owner will really learn to extract the best from his engine in different models.

The popularity of four-strokes has led at least one manufacturer to start making a range of propellers which have been computer designed for this type of engine. To date only two sizes are available but this will increase and other manufacturers must follow suit.

The final item required for operating any engine is the fuel tank. There are a wide range on the market and any commercial tank will work as well as any other.

The tank should be located with its centre line just below the level of the centre of the carb intake whenever possible. Sometimes this isn't possible because the carb is mounted on the cylinder head of the engine. Engines with this arrangement will either have sufficient suction for this not to be a problem, or will have some form of pressure to the tank. The unusual step of fitting a fuel pump to the engine may be taken, so far the British Condor is the only engine to adopt this method with an extremely simple but effective pump driven by a cam on the end of the rotary valve in the cylinder head.

The Enya timing chest dismantled showing the twin camshafts, cam followers and pushrods with their covers.

Saito 90T flat twin, engine is supplied with comprehensive tool kit. Twin carbs take a little time to get used to but are very effective.

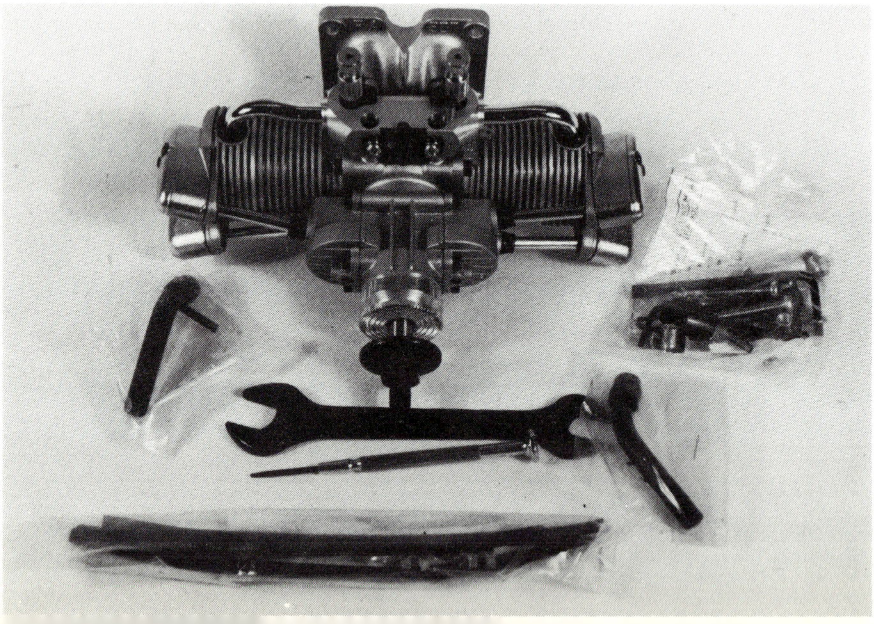

The low fuel consumption of the four-stroke means that a much smaller fuel tank can be used. A six ounce tank is more than adequate for the .45 cu.in. size engines and a four ounce tank will give up to 15 minutes flying with a .40 cu.in. engine. The small tank means that there is less change in the fuel feed throughout the run and of course means that there is more room in the tank bay so that locating the tank for optimum fuel feed is easier.

Fuel lines should be kept as short as possible as with any other engine. A fuel filter in the line is not recommended except where it is mentioned for the HP VT 21. This is because it can clog in flight giving rise to erratic running or leaning out of the mixture. It is far better to filter the fuel from the main container to the fuel container and again in the filler line from the fuel pump or in the squeeze bottle. Yes, with four-strokes using small tanks the old squeeze bottle is a cheap and useful method of filling the tank.

Apart from the items directly connected with the engine and its use, there is one other item that needs to be discussed and this is the lead from the battery to the glowplug.

The glowplug location on four-strokes varies far more than on any two-stroke. It may be at the rear of the head, at the side or facing forwards and it is often buried between rockerboxes or cylinder fins. Many of these locations will not accept the normal glowclip and the forward facing plugs will not accept the tubular type because the propeller gets in the way. Saito overcome this problem by providing a special clip-on lead which allows for remote connection of the plug. A similar connection can be made by soldering the female half of a press stud to the glow lead but this will not fit all plugs. The author uses a home made connector for the plug post which is simply a piece of brass tube flattened over half its length and soldered to the wire, the flattened end is bent as shown in Fig.3 and a piece of fuel tube slipped over the whole thing. This tube insulates the metal parts and holds the connector to the plug post, the other wire can be connected to any part of the engine.

Detonation, knocking or pinking can develop when running a four-stroke badly. This is a heavy note to the exhaust and may sound like a mechanical knock. If it is really bad it can make the engine backfire and throw the propeller and its nut completely off the crankshaft. It may develop as the throttle is opened from the idle position or when adjusting the needle valve and is caused by any one or more of several factors. Too big a propeller, too high a Nitromethane content in the fuel, too high a compression ratio or too weak a mixture. If detonation occurs in flight, shut the throttle at once, if it happens on the ground open the needle valve and if that does not cure it stop the engine. Detonation and the cures are covered in depth in the chapter on faults.

O.S. FS 80. O.S. are unusual in that they use both front and rear mounted camshafts. On this engine one can remove the front housing for inspection. — Irvine Engines photo.

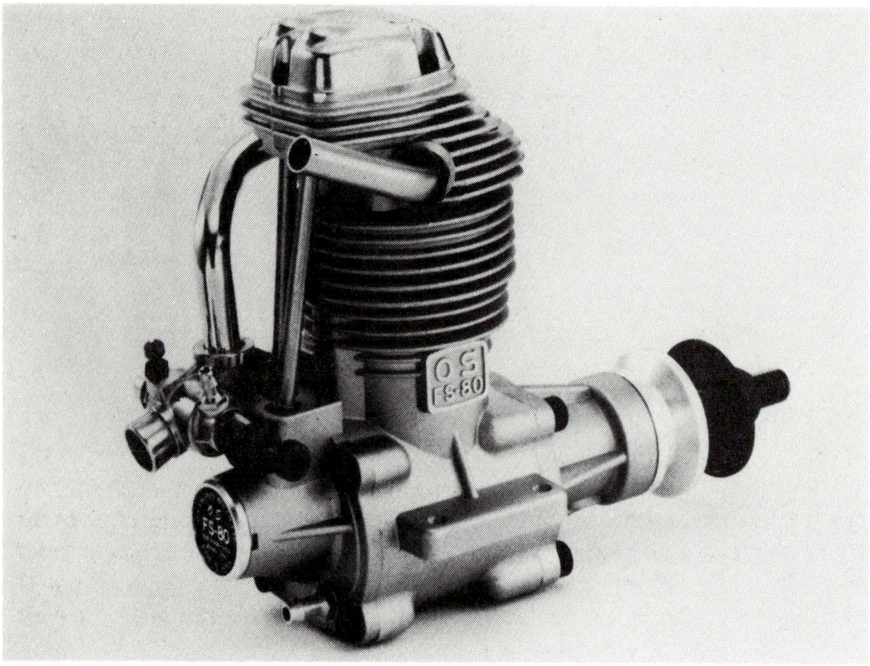

O.S. FS 40. On this engine the rear cover can be removed for inspection.

Chapter 5

Maintenance and Fault Finding

Considering the extra complexity of the four-stroke, with four times as many moving parts as the two-stroke, they are very reliable engines. To illustrate this point, the author has flown a large number of different engines and accumulated several hundred running hours with them. In all this time there have been two component failures, one fault and two lost parts which were due to lack of care on the author's part. The detailed list is given below:

One valve spring failed during running in
One exhaust pipe cracked round the flange
One leaking manifold
One lost pushrod after a crash, should have been seen on the spot
One exhaust pipe and nut fell off in flight, not tight enough.

Two faults were avoidable, one was easily cured, while the exhaust pipe was easily replaced. Only the broken valve spring involved any real dismantling of the engine. Slight traces of corrosion have been found on one of the first engines used but all the others have been protected after each flying session and no further problems have been found.

Like any precision machine the engines do need looking after and a little regular maintenance will keep the engine in perfect condition at the cost of about ten minutes work after each flying session.

The first thing that has to be said is: don't take your engine to pieces just to see what it looks like inside. Only dismantle an engine if it needs repairs and then only take off the essential items needed to reach the parts that need changing. If the engine is still under guarantee send it back anyway and if you are not completely confident that you can take an intricate machine apart and put it together again, send it back to the

Saito T 240 is an impressive engine, it follows the Saito practice of using two cylinders from one of their single cylinder engines to build a twin, in this case the cylinders come from the .120 cu.in. engine. — Macgregor photo.

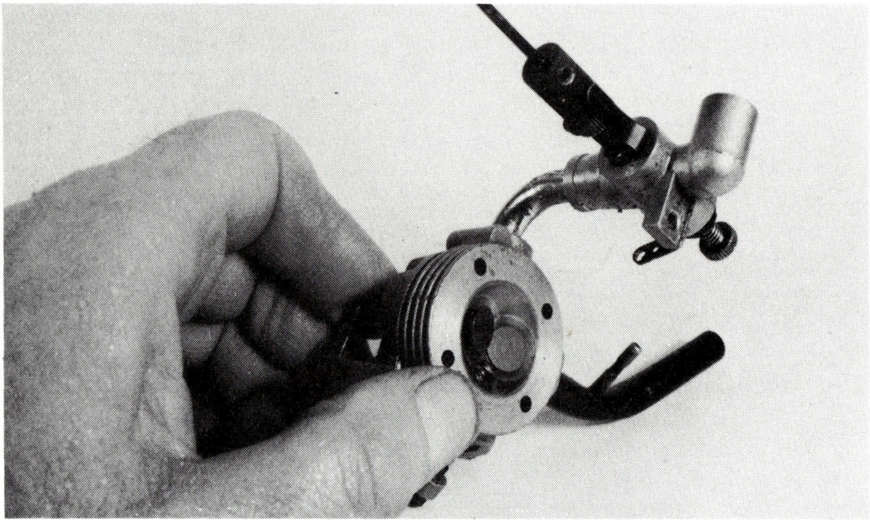

Saito FA 40 head showing intake valve open. Manifold between carb and cylinderhead must be sealed at both ends as air leaks will cause erratic running, this applies to all four-strokes with manifolds.

service agent. It will be cheaper in the long run.

There are only two items that need to be done on a regular basis. After each session oiling, and checking the tappet clearances.

After every running or flying session a good, light machine oil such as 3-in-1 oil should be injected through the breather nipple in the crankcase and the engine held so that the oil can flow through the lower part of the engine and especially the crankshaft bearings, camshafts and gears. On the HP VT engines oil should also be injected through the nipple in the cylinder head. HP recommend draining this oil out and putting fresh oil in to be really sure that the engine is properly flushed out while running in. This oiling should still be carried out even when an anti-corrosion inhibitor is added to the fuel. As the breather nipple is often difficult to reach, a length of tubing should be fitted, this will also allow the oil pumped out by the engine to be carried clear of the model in flight.

Enya engines have a very small hole in the end of the nipple, the author always drills these out with a 1/16th drill as it makes the after session oiling much easier.

Engines with exposed rocker arms and pushrods should have these parts checked for dirt or grit and then oiled as they get no other lubrication. Engines with enclosed valve gear do get some lubrication but Saito provide a special grease for the rockers and this should be applied as needed. Check this when checking the tappet clearances.

The tappet clearances are the gaps between the pad on the rocker arm and the valve stem. The instructions will give the correct clearance for the engine and normally a feeler gauge is provided with the other tools that come with the engine. The O.S. FS-60 has no clearance, so one must be careful that the rocker is only just touching the valve stem and not actually pushing it down or there will be a loss of compression and possibly a burnt valve.

Tappet clearances should be checked after each half hour of running for the first hour and then about once every flying hour after that, but it will be found that actual clearances do not change for several hours. However, just because the clearances have not changed for some time don't forget about them, they will change and the result will be some power loss. A sudden change in the gaps can be a warning of wear taking place in the valve mechanism. Engines with rotary valves do not have tappet clearances to worry about.

Tappet clearances on model four-strokes are always set with the engine cold, this ensures a standard setting and the designer has taken into account the expansion due to heat in the various parts of the engine. If the tappets are set with the engine hot the clearances will certainly be wrong and could even cause damage.

The procedure for setting the clearances is straightforward but may

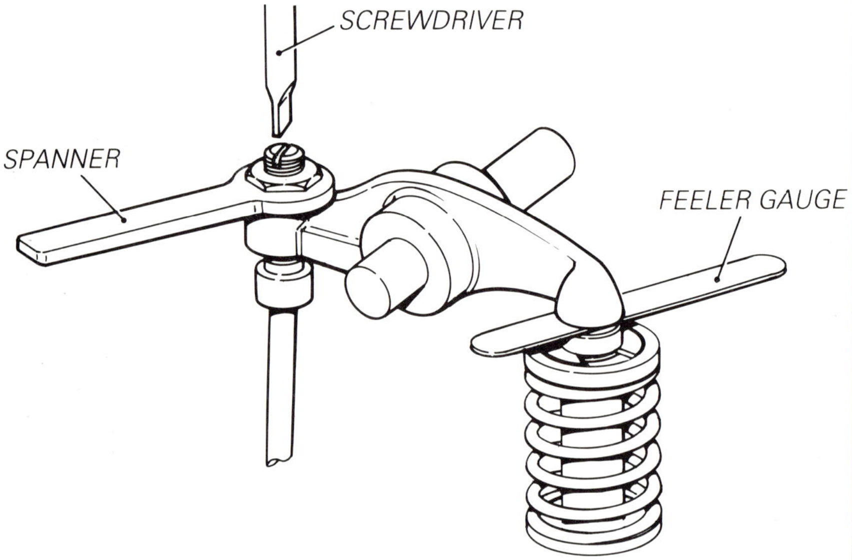

SETTING VALVE CLEARANCES

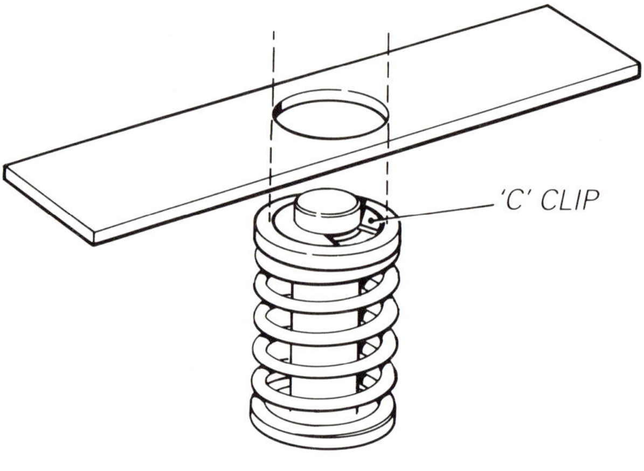

VALVE SPRING COMPRESSOR

take a little practice to get used to.

First, to check the clearance the valves should be positioned in accordance with the engine instructions or, if these have been lost or the engine is second hand with no instructions, the position can be found by turning the engine over until the valve is fully open. At this position moving the propeller in either direction will alllow the valve to start closing. Now turn the propeller one complete turn and this will give the maximum valve clearance ready for checking.

Using a feeler gauge is very easy but like all things there is a knack to it. The gauge must be slipped into the gap and allowed to align itself, because a gauge that is held out of true with the gap will give the impression that the gap is tight when it could be quite wide.. Take a little time just trying the fit until you are used to it, later it will be a very quick operation. The gauge should be able to move with just the slightest friction and there should be no movement felt on the rocker arm. If the fit is such that any effort is needed to move the gauge the gap is too small.

To set the tappet clearance slacken the adjuster locking nut, this will often unscrew the adjuster slightly, this is not important as the gap is to be reset anyway. Now fit the feeler gauge in the gap and gently screw in the adjuster until the gauge is gripped very lightly. Test the amount of friction and when you are happy with the setting hold the adjusting screw in position with a screwdriver and tighten the locking nut firmly. Finally re-check the friction on the gauge in case the action of tightening the locking nut has altered the setting. The whole operation will not take more than a couple of minutes for each tappet clearance.

Most engines specify a tappet clearance of 0.08mm or 0.1mm or 0.0015 to 0.004in, so if the engine is not new and the feeler gauge provided is missing one can buy a set at any motor accessory shop.

One other check that is worth while is to make sure that all the screws are tight and any exhaust nuts are not working loose.

These days most four-strokes are assembled with Allen screws, also known as hexagon socket head screws, and Allen keys are provided with the engine. Use these with care, an Allen key allows far more leverage to be applied to a screw and it is quite easy to strip a thread in aluminium. The small size of most Allen keys allows some spring in the key to be felt, when this springiness is felt the screw should be tight enough and any more pressure will either strip the thread, bend the key or chew the flats out of the sockethead. This just about takes care of regular maintenance requirements of the four-stroke.

It has already been shown that faults are few and far between on four-strokes but there are a number of potential faults that could arise, some of these may need one or more of various possible cures while others may be difficult to diagnose but most will be fairly easy to cure.

The most likely fault to be encountered is called "Detonation" where the fuel does not burn but literally explodes, this makes the engine run very heavily with a knocking sound. Very often detonation can kick the propeller loose and it will cause rapid wear to the engine, especially the connecting rod bearings and main bearings. Under some circumstances detonation may occur when the throttle is opened quickly from the idle position.

There are several causes of detonation, mixture too weak, propeller too big, too much nitromethane in the fuel, the compression ratio too high or plug too hot. Nitromethane and compression ratio are interlinked, the higher the compression ratio the less nitromethane should be used. Enya four-strokes provide an extra cylinder head gasket for use with large propellers or high nitro fuels. The Enya 35-4C did not have this gasket while the instructions recommended 15% nitromethane. In fact the engine was much better on straight fuel when used with a large propeller and making an 0.008in. aluminium gasket allowed the use of 5% nitro in the fuel on a 12 x 5in. prop.

When detonation occurs in flight, shut the throttle at once and land. If the detonation is apparent when the throttle is opened quickly closing the throttle and then opening it slowly will help but the main cause must still be rectified on landing. Opening the needle valve may be enough to cure the problem, if not, try a smaller propeller or use a fuel with lower nitromethane content.

Fully cowled engines may suffer from detonation if there is insufficient cooling flow through the cowl. One problem with detonation is that it generates extra heat which makes the detonation worse and so on *ad infinitum*.

Another cause of detonation could be a carbon build up in the cylinder head. This would only apply to engines that had seen a great deal of use and the most carbon build up seen so far is a small amount on the stem of the exhaust valve.

Fuel feed problems are the same as those suffered by two-stroke engines. Trouble can come from the tank being too far away from the engine or too high or too low, holes in the fuel line letting in air and fuel blockages or partial blockages. The normal check of setting the needle valve and then holding the model nose high should be carried out. If the engine leans out, open the needle valve. If it is found to be impossible to set the needle valve on the ground and get consistent engine runs in flight it may be the tank position but there is another possible fault which can be tested easily, an air leak in the intake manifold. The test for this is to run the engine on the ground and dribble fuel over the manifold where it enters the carburettor and cylinder head. If the engine runs rich for a few moments, there is a leak but be sure that no fuel has entered the air intake as this will give the same effect when in fact there is no leak present.

If a leak is found at either end of the manifold the carburettor will have to be removed and the "O" rings examined for damage. Some engines have the "O" ring at the head end of the manifold recessed into the end of th manifold. This "O" ring should stand slightly proud of the end of the manifold. If it has squashed down it must be replaced.

If there is no visible damage to the "O" rings, the fault may be caused through incorrect assembly of the manifold. This must be pressed firmly home in the cylinder head before the grubscrew is tightened. If the grubscrew has previously been tightened to the extent that a mark has been made in the manifold there is a danger that retightening the screw will cause it to try and slip back into the indentation and so moving the manifold out again. Here the cure is to clean off any such indentation with a small fine file. An emergency repair on the flying field may be carried out with either a little 5 minute epoxy or Cyanoacrylate glue. The oil in the area will prevent a permanent joint being made and allow the glue to be cleaned off later when a permanent repair is carried out. After repairing an air leak repeat the test of dribbling fuel over the manifold joints to make sure that the repair has been successful.

The most likely area for any mechanical failure is in the valve gear. Engines with exposed valves and rockers etc. are the easiest one to check, they are also the type that is most likely to suffer in a heavy landing. After any landing where the model has run into grass or any other obstruction it is vital to examine the pushrods before moving the model. It is quite easy for a pushrod to be dislodged and then the cam follower can fall out of the timing chest. If the model is inspected before moving it the chances are very good that any missing parts can be found close by. Most engine manufacturers are going over to fully enclosed valve gear which is a good thing.

If a four-stroke stops suddenly and is found to have lost all compression there are three likely faults. A valve spring has broken or the valve stem has snapped or the retaining device come off the valve stem. In the event of the spring breaking there will probably be no other damage but if the valve has dropped into the cylinder as would happen in either of the other two failures there may be damage to the piston, cylinder and head. If the valve has dropped do not turn the engine over as more damage will be caused.

One other type of valve failure that will give the same symptons is a bent valve stem. This will almost certainly be caused by the piston hitting the valve and is almost always caused by excessive r.p.m. This used to be a common fault in racing cars and motorcycles. Using a propeller smaller than the minimum recommended by the engine manufacturer could cause the same problem with model engines but it must be said that it would take quite a substantial case of overspeeding to reach this stage.

Apart from one broken valve spring the author has not heard of any case of valve failure, however with the large numbers of four-strokes in use there will eventually be some failures and it is as well to know the symptoms.

The dismantling and reassembly of a two-stroke engine is a relatively simple affair. In spite of this fact the author has, over the years, come across engines that have been incorrectly assembled and engines that have been "butchered" in the process. Some classic examples include cylinders assembled back to front, contra-pistons in diesels fitted upside down and cylinder heads that have been distorted by incorrect tightening of the bolts. If these mistakes can be made with the simple two-stroke consider the scope for messing up a four-stroke. The moral is: unless you feel completely confident in your skills do not try to do any major dismantling of your four-stroke engine, send it back to the maker or service agent.

Having said that, it is worth discussing various degrees of disassembly on the two main types of four-strokes i.e. poppet valve and rotary valve engines.

The rotary valve engine is the easier of the two to work on as it has very few extra parts. The poppet valve engine is much more likely to present problems.

Before any work is started a clean surface such as an old worktop or at the very least a large sheet of clean white paper is needed. Also some small containers and all the tools that will be needed and the engine instructions which should give details of the timing of the valves and any other special instructions, such as the method of resealing the crankcase on the HP VT engines.

The inspection of the bottom end of the engine for corrosion is one of the most likely reasons for working on an engine and is very basic in most cases. Where an engine has the camshaft in front of the cylinder the backplate can be removed while if the camshaft is at the rear of the engine it is normally possible to remove the front housing and crankshaft. These operations can be done without disturbing the timing. On the HP VT engines the bottom half of the crankcase has to be removed and this will disturb the timing of the valve, however this is fairly simple to re-set. The piston is brought to top dead centre (TDC) and the rotary valve is fitted so that an equal amount of the valve port can be seen in the exhaust port and the inlet port. If the propeller driver has not been removed from the crankshaft there is a small timing mark on this which, when aligned with the top web on the crankcase, indicates that the piston is at TDC.

Removal of the cylinder head from a rotary valve engine will disturb the valve timing. The valve cover at the top may be removed without affecting anything, but if the engine is turned over with the cover removed and a glowplug fitted, the valve will be lifted out by compression and the timing setting lost, but this can be re-set as described above.

Removal of the cylinder head from a poppet valve engine will not affect the timing, the only points to note is that the push rods will come out and care must be taken to fit them properly on reassembly. It is good practice to make sure that the push rods and any other valve parts are always fitted to the same valve that they came from.

A good way to test the valves for any slight leakage when the head is removed is to support the cylinder head upsidedown in a level position and fill it with paraffin and watch for any drips from the ports.

On full size engines the valves can be ground in to cure any slight leaks, the normal method is to remove the valve spring and then, using a piece of dowel with a rubber suction cup on it, the valve is rotated against its seat with some grinding paste. While this has not been tried on a model engine it should be possible but using metal polish rather than grinding paste. Make sure that every trace of metal polish is removed before re-assembling the engine and remember, if you mess it up, cylinder heads are expensive.

The removal and refitting of poppet valves is one of the fiddly jobs on a four-stroke. The valves are held closed by a spring, this spring usually operates against a large washer on the valve stem and this washer is held in place by one of several methods. It may be held by an "E" clip which is a type of circlip, it may be held by a proper circlip or it may follow full size practice and use very tiny split collets which seat in a groove in the valve stem and a recess in the washer.

Before deciding to remove the valves remember that they are spring loaded and that one slip at the wrong moment will send various tiny parts across the room. If, after considering this, it is decided that the valve will be taken out of the head, proceed with caution.

The room should be relatively uncluttered, a workshop full of balsa shavings, dust and half finished models is no place to have to look for small parts. (Bitter experience talking.) It is a good idea to try and work in a cardboard box if possible.

The valve to be removed must have its head rested against something firm, a small block of wood that will press against it will do. Then the washer on the valve stem must be pressed down compressing the spring and the circlip or collets removed and the spring tension slowly released and the valve can now be removed. Reassembly is the reverse procedure but an extra pair of hands is a great help.

No special tools are commercially available for compressing the spring but a simple and easily made tool could be a strip of metal with a hole drilled in one end. This hole should be large enough for the circlip or collets to pass through but not the washer. When split collets are used, a small pair of tweezers are a great help when it comes to putting them back.

There should be no need to dismantle the cam shafts on any engine unless the cams have worn badly, which is unlikely, or corrosion has attacked the bearings or camshaft in which case a service department rebuild of the engine would be the sensible thing to have done. Most engine instructions do give the correct way to re-time the engine and provide timing marks on the cam gears or equivalent. Some engines do not give any instructions for retiming the engine. O.S. engines do not and the O.S. instructions suggest returning the engine for any work on the camshaft. One such job mentioned is the fitting of a reverse rotation camshaft on some of their engines. This would be for twin engined models or for a pusher layout using normal propellers.

The most important stage in working on an engine is the re-assembly. It is essential that everything is spotlessly clean, that any damaged gaskets are replaced. (It is good policy to fit new gaskets anyway but not vital.)

If a gasket is damaged and no spares are to hand it is quite easy to make one. Most small engineering shops and all maintenance departments in factories will keep a range of gasket papers of various thicknesses and will usually be helpful if approached. Take part of the engine along so that they can see what you are doing, also take the old gasket so that the correct thickness paper can be selected.

Once you have the paper, making the gasket is a few minutes work. First smear a thin layer of oil or grease on the face where the gasket is to be fitted. A very thin coat is all that is needed, any more will spread too much. Now press the gasket paper against the oiled face and when it is removed a perfect image of the gasket should be visible. Cut round this with a sharp modelling knife, punch out any holes with brass tubing sharpened with a knife and the gasket is made.

Tightening down bolts should be done progressively so that each one is loaded equally. Work in a diagonal pattern, i.e., assuming a six bolt head, numbered clockwise from 1 to 6, the sequence would be: 1, 4, 2, 5, 3, 6 and so on.

All parts should be given a thin coating of oil before re-assembly and each part should be checked for freedom of movement after it has been fitted. A careful check made for leaks after the cylinder head has been fitted is essential. The final check after any work on the engine is to make sure that the tappet clearances are correct.

When any work has been completed it is a good idea to bench run the engine or failing that, run a tankful of fuel through the engine at a rich setting to help everything bed down again.

The last word in this chapter is to repeat the warning. Don't take your engine to pieces unless it is vital and you are confident that you know what you are doing.

Close up of the cowling on the Sig Piper Cub, the rocker box of the O.S. FS 40 is very unobtrusive and could be mistaken for part of the full size engine.

O.S. FS 40 fitted to the author's Sig Piper Cub. In this case there was enough room to use a normal clevis on the throttle arm.

Chapter 6

Installing the Four-Stroke

Fitting a four-stroke engine to a model is not difficult but there are various factors that do have to be considered, so models designed for two-strokes may need some modification, with throttle runs and connections calling for some thought. Of course the small exhaust pipe and silencer does simplify matters in that there are no great big "dustbins" to hide or find space for.

There are a few modellers who have expressed interest at seeing the author's models with side mounted and inverted engines, so let's get that one out of the way first. A four-stroke can be mounted any way up that suits the model without any problems. In fact, an inverted four-stroke is less liable to flood than a two-stroke because the exhaust valve allows surplus fuel to drain out, but it is vital that the engine is turned over slowly by hand to make sure that there is no hydraulic lock as the engine comes up to compression. If a lock is found the engine should be turned over in a clockwise direction (backwards) to allow the excess fuel to be ejected through the exhaust valve. The same applies to a side mounted engine but this is less likely to flood. Because there is no port open at the bottom of the stroke, an upright engine is liable to flooding and locking, which is the direct opposite of a two-stroke. However, the normal location of the carburettor helps to reduce this and again, the excess fuel can be ejected by flicking the engine over by hand. The author never uses an electric starter and has never felt the need for one on any engine, including control line speed models. There can be no doubt that hand flicking an engine will tell the experienced operator a great deal about the state of the engine and how near it is to starting, whether it is flooded or starved of fuel, but this experience can only be gained

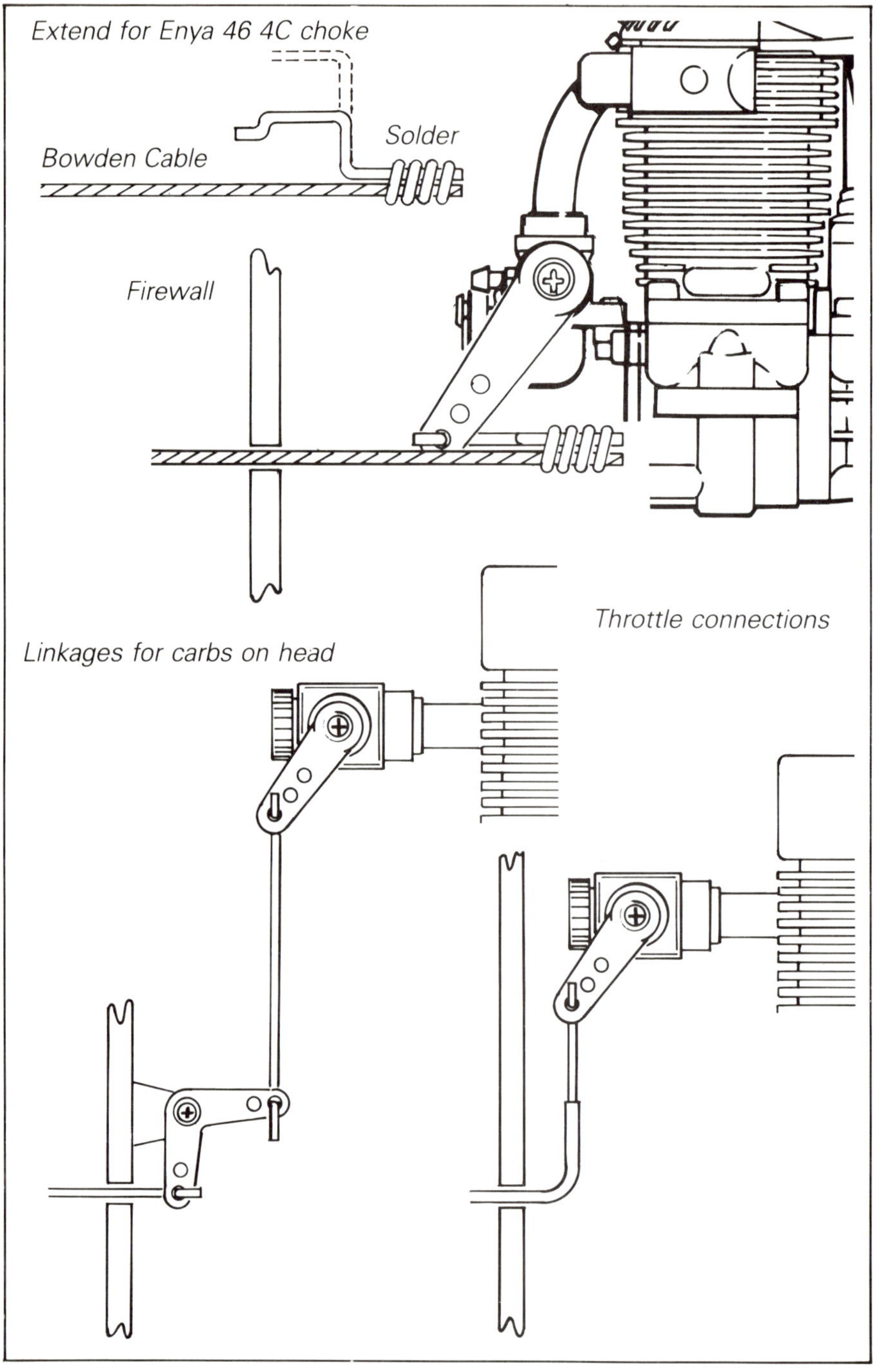
Extend for Enya 46 4C choke
Solder
Bowden Cable
Firewall
Throttle connections
Linkages for carbs on head

through constant handstarting.

The average four-stroke is considerably longer than most two-strokes. This is because usually the carburettor and sometimes the valve mechanism is at the rear of the engine. This puts two requirements on the model, first, the engine bearers have to be longer and so they will be more flexible. Where wooden bearers are used, a slight increase in size is a good idea. Commercial engine mounts are quite satisfactory, aluminium ones being preferred. Fortunately there is a steadily increasing range of such mounts suitable for four-strokes coming onto the market.

The second effect of the longer four-stroke is to move the centre of mass of the engine forward. This is not a good thing because the four-stroke is already heavier than a two-stroke and so the balance point will be moved forward. This can be an advantage on some scale models but not on the average sports type, which was originally designed for a two-stroke. Some lead may be needed in the tail to compensate for the extra weight and nose length, and weights at either end of a model are not going to help the flight characteristics in any way. The answer is to move the front bulkhead or firewall back to keep the engine in the correct place, or shorten the nose of the model.

Moving the firewall back will shorten the tank bay, but the economy of the four-stroke will still allow long flights on the smaller tank that may have to be fitted.

The four-strokes which do not have rear mounted carburettors or valve gear will not need an engine bay any longer than the average two-stroke but some, the HP VT 49 for one, are very heavy and this will need to be allowed for.

Throttle control runs are another area where some thought will pay dividends. The engines with front mounted carburettors can be treated as normal two-strokes but engines with rear mounted carburettors need special but simple linkages. Due to the closeness of the carb. to the firewall, there will rarely be room for a normal clevis or ball link. The author uses a metal bowden cable with a wire "Joggle" soldered on which is the most compact way of making the connection. All adjustment is done at the servo end of the cable.

Engines which have the carburettor coming straight out of the cylinder head will need a linkage designed to suit the installation. Where the head is exposed an external linkage may be the only answer but if the throttle arm can be moved to any position, it may be possible to arrange a cable to sweep through a right angle to connect to the arm, thus hiding the control run. An alternative would be an idler bellcrank in the engine compartment.

Some engines may need even more thought for the throttle linkage,

The Webra .40 4-T fitted to the author's Super Scorpion, note the square finning and belt cover, also high tank location.

The O.S. FS 40 fitted to a Veron Hawker Tomtit. Four-strokes are ideal for this type of model and the cylinder blends well with the dummy cylinders. — Tony Stephenson photo.

an example is the Enya 46-4C. This engine has a choke system which involves pulling the carb barrel including the throttle arm sideways. As this will be close to the firewall, some provision must be made for this sideways movement of the arm. The simplest answer is to use the joggle but to make the part that goes through the throttle arm about ¼in. long, allowing the arm to slide along it as the choke is pulled out.

When installing a four-stroke a length of silicone tube should be fitted to the crankcase breather to carry the ejected oil out of the cowling and clear of the aircraft. This will also serve another important function, making it easier to pump oil into the crankcase after each flying session, a vital step if corrosion is to be avoided. If such a pipe is not fitted it will be difficult to get to the breather nipple and when one is tired there will be a temptation to leave it till later.

The HP VT engines have a different arrangement in that the exhaust gasses are taken from the silencer to the head and then travel down to the crankcase and along the crankshaft to a nipple which is connected to the tank. This lubricates the valve gears, pressurises the tank and takes the excess oil back to the tank. There is also a drain plug in the crankcase which has to be removed to flush out the engine after the first few runs. Because of all this plumbing it is important that the cowlings will permit access to the whole of the crankcase. (See VT21 engine test report.)

Access to the carburettor should be considered on engines with rear mounted carbs as these are in a restricted area at the best of times although, once set up, there should be little need to adjust them. However, if you can't reach it, it will be bound to need attention.

The easiest part of installation will be the exhaust as the pipe can normally be swivelled through 360° and any silencer is on the end of the exhaust pipe. In most cases a small hole or slot in the cowling will suffice and it is very simple to extend the pipe with a length of silicone tubing. The silencer on the HP VT 21 is fixed directly to the cylinder head on a short stub which is part of the silencer but it can be rotated to any position and is a very small silencer about ¼in. diameter.

Cooling is an important factor for any engine and especially so for a four-stroke. On a two-stroke there is a constant cooling flow of fresh mixture through the crankcase and the hot exhaust gases are rapidly released towards the bottom of the power stroke. The four-stroke has a closed crankcase and the hot gasses remain in the cylinder for the whole of the power stroke-exhaust stroke.

Over heating can lead to detonation, which will generate more heat and possibly also lead to damage of valves and wear out bearings. Engines are designed to run at the correct temperature even when completely exposed to the airstream, so any serious reduction in the airflow

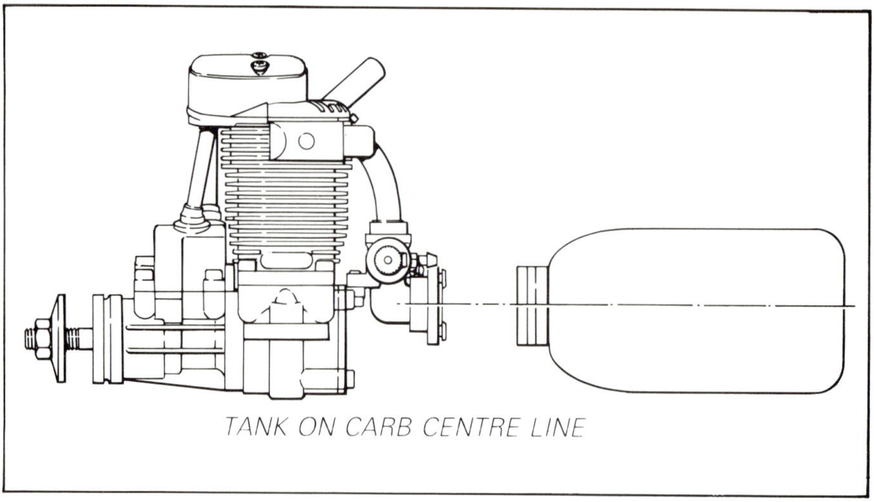

The German made Jupiter 37cc twin O.H.C., this is the underside of the engine. Belt drive to the rotary valve is visible.
Jupiter also make an 18.5cc single. — Wik-Model photo.

can lead to overheating.

For adequate cooling there must be an air intake which will direct the air over the cooling fins, there should also be a stream of air over the crankcase. Two or three ¼in. holes will help in the latter instance.

The rocker box may be exposed in many installations due to the extra height of the four-stroke. If it is enclosed, then there should be a space between the rocker box and the cowl. It is also good practice with any engine to fit baffles so that the air is forced between the cooling fins, although it must be admitted that few designs feature this and the engines still run perfectly well.

Just as important as air intakes are the air outlets. The air expands as it is heated by the engine and so larger outlets are needed, a total of 1½ to 2 times the intake area is often quoted. Very large intakes, as in radial cowlings, do not need outlets of the same ratio but they should still be as large as possible. On models where the cylinder head protrudes through the cowling, some of the outlet can be round the head. Leaving a gap of 3/16in. all round is one way, alternatively leaving a gap behind the cylinder back to the firewall is good as it will tend to make the air flow round the back of the cylinder, this also allows access to the plumbing and is not too noticeable.

Because of the extra height of the four-stroke, the average modeller rarely fits one to any of the close cowled scale types such as the Spitfire. However, it is worth mentioning that some successful scale models have been flown with watercooled two-strokes and this would be worth experimenting with.

Four-stroke glowplugs are normally sharply angled within the head compared to two-strokes. In some engines they are even horizontal and on the side of the head, but in the majority of cases they are between the rocker arms or extend forwards while a few are at the rear of the cylinder head. Those at the side or rear of the head present few problems, but those facing forward are not so simple and the best answer is to fit a lead to a small plug or metal part of the model such as the undercarriage. Alternatively there are special remote plug connector harnesses available which are reasonably priced and save the time and effort involved in making up a similar item. They will also have purpose designed plug connectors which are not available elsewhere, but the connector described in Chapter 4 does work very well.

Careful installation of the engine will save a lot of headaches and will be repaid with better peformance and longer life of the engine.

One of the best .60 four strokes is the Laser 61. Rolls Royce technology goes into this engine, which is machined from solid.

Chapter 7

Selecting a Model for your Engine

There are a number of kits specially designed for four-stroke engines on the market and a lot of kit manufacturers are now putting two-stroke and four-stroke power ranges on their kit boxes. Unfortunately some of the latter kits are just not suitable for four-stroke engines, this leads to modellers feeling that four-strokes are no use or lack power when, in fact, it is the model that is wrong for the engine.

Let us compare how the two types of engine deliver their power. The two-stroke is a high revving engine turning a small propeller, if loaded down with a large propeller it will drop well below its peak power and become inefficient. The two-stroke likes fast models but will fly the slower types.

The four-stroke develops its peak power at much lower r.p.m. but turning a large propeller. It will not fly a fast model because it cannot achieve the high r.p.m. needed. There are one or two exceptions to this rule, notably the HP VT engines but even here the VT 49 likes a large propeller.

From the above it will be seen that the obvious choice will be the slower type of aircraft, which does not necessarily mean very slow "floaters" but aircraft which can fly slowly, or to put it more precisely aircraft with a low stalling speed. If the model has a high stalling speed the gap between the stall and maximum speed will be small and this will mean that it will be liable to fall out of the sky if the speed is lost.

All vintage models come into the low stalling speed category and as most vintage models have a short nose the extra weight of the four-stroke is helpful in getting the balance point in the right place without having to add lead to the nose. Vintage models also make very good trainers because if the student pilot gets into trouble the transmitter sticks can be released and the model will sort itself out and regain level flight after which the pilot can take over again. This method of learning will give the novice time to think and time to learn about flying and reduces the stress factor. The hardest part of learning is landing and here the vintage model helps again as it will land itself and the pilot need only concentrate on steering the model so that it lands roughly where he wants it.

The four-stroke is also a natural choice for scale models but selection of a subject is more important. Most World War I aircraft are suitable for four-strokes as many had rotary engines with large cowlings and short noses. The large propeller used by four-strokes and their weight are both advantages here. Even the in-line engined types such as the SE5 and Fokker DVII will benefit from this type of engine

Most WWI aircraft were built up and fabric covered and so were quite light. All were comparatively low powered, in spite of having quite large engines.

The same factors that make the WWI aircraft suitable subjects also apply to aircraft between the wars, especially civil types. The Gypsy type of engine powered most British aircraft and these lend themselves to four-stroke power to perfection. Many American civil aircraft used radial engines and here again the four-stroke is an excellent match, the Saito range will blend into a scale radial engine very well indeed.

Most British fighters used in-line engines combined with very sleek cowlings and these aircraft present problems in hiding the engine. Half the different types of American fighters used radial engines and the four-stroke is again a very suitable engine, while Japanese aircraft could have been designed to produce simple scale installations.

WWII aircraft are less suitable for four-stroke engines although several very successful and convincing models have been built for this type of engine but the larger engines are better for the purpose.

The large range of post-war light planes and some of the piston powered military types are suited to four-stroke power, but the best type of post war aircraft for four-strokes are the vast number of homebuilt designs. Many of these are powered by Volkswagen engines and are relatively slow and lightly loaded.

Some aircraft, which could be powered by four-strokes, lose all the character of the full size when so powered. The Pitts Special and North American Harvard are two that spring to mind as these aircraft have a particularly hard crackly sound in flight. The Pitts also needs a lot of power for aerobatics and the stalling speed tends to be on the high side.

Looking now at the non-scale models, the four-stroke is being experimented with for aerobatics. The "turn around" aerobatic schedule calls for a slower aircraft which can be flown in a small area of the sky. For sport flying some of the aerobatic models of the 50s and 60s are excellent, these models spanning up to 72in. were flown in competition with heavy radio equipment and engines in the .35 to .45 cu.in. range and those engines did not develop the power of equivalent sized engines today. An Astro Hog or Gee String with a 60 cu.in. four-stroke is a beautiful model to fly and there were many other such designs.

The models designed in the 50s and 60s did not use foam wings or fibreglass fuselages and had to be built lightly, they did not rely on brute power to haul them around and so they would all fly slowly if need be. These old designs should be a happy hunting ground for the four-stroke owner.

With the popularity of four-strokes there are an increasing number of plans being published specifically for this type of engine, these designs cover all types of model from scale through sports models to fully aerobatic types, there are even some trainers. There are also kits covering all sizes of engine and these will increase in number and variety.

As a rough guide to deciding if a kit is suitable for a four-stroke engine one can check on the various points that will affect performance and installation. The wing loading for models in the .21 to .60 cu.in. range should be under 24 ounces per square foot, ideally 20 oz per sq. ft. but the higher figure is acceptable. The nose should be comparatively short or should be capable of being modified and the engine bay must be capable of taking the extra length of the engine or, again should be capable of modification. Less important but still helpful, the wing section should be semi-symmetrical or even flat bottomed, if the wing loading is at the top end of the scale this becomes more important. Reading the flight test reports in this book will help with the decision.

The pointers indicate the areas where air leaks might occur on a manifold.

Saito include a neat glass-bowl filter amongst their accessories.

Chapter 8

Model Design for Four-Strokes

Designing a model for four-stroke power units is very similar to any other design but there are certain factors which are of greater importance if the model is to be a pleasure to fly. The most important of these is the wing loading.

Let us begin with some very simple and basic truths about aerodynamics. For the basic example take a model with a wing loading of 20 ounces per sq.ft. Assume that it is designed so that when all controls and trims are neutral and the throttle is set at half power the model will fly straight and level. Now, any increase in wing loading by exceeding the design weight will cause the model to lose height given the half power/neutral controls. To compensate, either the angle of attack must be increased and the speed will drop, or more power must be applied. If the wing loading is increased enough, the angle of attack will *have* to be increased, causing more drag until the model stalls or the throttle is opened to counteract the drag. Alternatively the power can be increased until the model is flying at full throttle when any further increase in wing loading will require greater angles of attack. From all this it can be seen that it is possible for a model to have such a high wing loading that it cannot fly. The only answer is a bigger engine.

It is unlikely but not impossible for a model to be built with such a high wing loading and this would be safer than a model with a wing loading that just allows it to fly, i.e. if it can't fly it can't crash.

The model which can *just* fly is dangerous, because any sudden increase in drag, such as a control input, can cause it to stall, while a sudden drop in wind speed on the approach will make the model drop suddenly. Forget the old story that "the model does not know there is any wind", wind does not have a constant speed and the model cannot change speed as quickly as the wind can. The heavier the model, the longer it takes to accelerate or decelerate when the wind speed changes.

A four-stroke engine runs at lower r.p.m. than most two-strokes, the propeller is often fairly fine pitch and large in diameter and so speeds are comparatively slow to start with. The higher the wing loading the smaller the gap in speed between climbing, level flight, descending and stalling and so the smaller the safety margin. Conversely, the bigger the gap the safer the model and low wing loading is the only way to increase the speed range. All this is just to explain the most important point in four-stroke model design, keep it light.

Just to press the point once more, an early Saito 30 would give enough power to loop and roll a Keil Kraft Super 60 weighing 5 lbs, that is a wing loading of about 18 ounces per sq.ft.

Four-stroke powered models need be no smaller than the models powered by the same capacity two-stroke engine so long as they have a lower wing loading.

The aerodynamic proportions of the model can be the same as a two-stroke model. If the engine is a particularly heavy one, the nose should be shortened to avoid having to put lead in the tail or make a heavy tail assembly, all of which is wasted weight.

Tail assemblies should be built up from strip and ribs even if they are of flat plate section. 3/8 x 1/2in. strips with 3/32in. ribs are quite strong enough, but a sheet fin may be used to give sufficient strength to cope with the model going over on its back.

Some of the greatest weight saving can be made in the fuselage, 3/32in. sheet sides, or even 1/16in. can be used with a framework of 1/4 x 1/8in. longerons and uprights. 1/32in. ply doublers will add plenty of strength. Completely built up fuselages, frames with stringers on all four sides, are quite successful instead of sheet. Ply formers can be cut away leaving just the stress bearing areas. Sizes given are for models up to .49 cu.in., .60 powered models can go up slightly in sizes.

Wing structures can follow conventional patterns but the ribs should be only 1/16in. sheet. Cap strips can be omitted and so can spar webs. This will make the wing slightly more flexible, not enough to upset the flight even in aerobatics but enough so that it will bend rather than snap in a crash. The Sig Piper Cub does not even have leading edge sheeting but the struts are fully functional and a very marked trim change will be noticed if a strut becomes detached in flight.

If a design is going to be very large for the engine size or will be heavy for reasons of complicated structures, a flat bottomed wing section would be an advantage. There are few sections of this type that will beat the good old Clark Y section. The author's Enya 40-4C powered 1/4 scale Polish homebuilt is a good example of this (see Enya 40-4C flight test report).

Great savings in weight can be made at the finishing stage. Solartex is about the strongest and lightest covering material and this can be sprayed with car touch up aerosols. By using the nearest colour of Solartex as a base, very little paint will be needed, the fuel proofer will give the gloss if required.

The figures for wing loading that should be aimed for are 20 ounces per sq.ft. for models up to .60 cu.in power. This figure will give good penetration and yet have a wide speed range and will allow most aerobatics. Higher wing loadings are acceptable but the aerobatic performance will be reduced. Anything over 24 ounces per sq.in. and a flat bottomed wing will help maintain the speed range but the speed range will decrease steadily as the loading gets higher.

Models powered by the larger engines can and do exceed these wing loadings quite safely, this can be accounted for by the greater efficiency of the larger model. Dave Platt has developed a theory that wing loadings should not be calculated on wing area but wing volume and his figures certainly prove that large models with very high wing loadings do in fact have similar loadings to the smaller models when calculated as volume loadings.

So much stress has been placed on the lightness of the model that many modellers may feel that the models will be very fragile. This just is not true when careful structural design work is done and the lighter models tend to bounce. The author's Turbulent has been flown into a tree (one broken propeller) flown into a scrap heap (one broken rudder hinge) and flown into a land draining machine (one small dent in the wing slot and a loosened tailplane). An Agro-Cat design has been cartwheeled in a ploughed field (no damage) and cartwheeled on landing overshoot (tailplane loosened). A much heavier model was blown over by the wind and had the tailplane break in two places. This proves that providing there are no sudden changes of section to create stress points and that the model can flex slightly, damage will be minimal.

Because of the great interest in four-strokes there is a large demand for planes that can be published in magazines both in this country and the USA. An attractive model that takes advantage of the four-stroke characteristics and is well proven will find a ready market and this can pay for a new engine or even a new set of radio equipment plus the tremendous satisfaction of seeing your own design in print.

The Magnum 91 was one of the first British four-strokes. 15cc capacity.

The FA-30 from Saito features exposed pushrods and rockers, which might cause problems of loss in a heavy landing.

Chapter 9

Flying a Four Stroke Powered Model

It may seem strange or superfluous to have this chapter in this book, especially as it has been said that four-strokes are not really recommended for the beginner. However, there will be modellers who are about to fly their first four-stroke powered model and it is worth pointing out a few of the differences, real and imagined.

When the silencer rule was first introduced modellers found that they were afraid to do any manoeuvres because the engine sounded as if it had no power. This feeling was particularly widespread in the control line field. Once the modeller had found the courage to do some basic aerobatics he found that he still had plenty of power and confidence was regained. In this case the frequency was unchanged, only the pitch or sound level was reduced.

Four-strokes only fire half as often as a two-stroke at any given r.p.m. and are also much quieter, so the feeling of having lost power is even stronger than was the case with two-strokes. It is a good idea to take this model up to a good height and throw it around, no need to do precise manoeuvres, just anything that comes to mind. From one manoeuvre go straight into another and in a very few minutes it will be found that one has regained confidence.

Another illusion created by the engine note is that the model is flying very slowly. Even low close passes seem slow because of the engine note. It is not until one tries to follow the model with a camera fitted with a telephoto lens that it is realised just how fast the model is travelling.

When flying a four-stroke powered model in the company of two-stroke powered models, the four-stroke will often be completely drowned out. The question is often heard: "Is it still running?". The only way to find out is to open the throttle for a moment to see if the nose rises or if a puff of smoke is given off from the exhaust. In situations like this it pays to be ready for a quick approach and landing as it is quite easy to be caught too low and too far out to make it back to the landing strip.

One area where the four-stroke has a great advantage over two-stroke models is that the model does not gain speed so rapidly in a vertical dive. It is interesting to note that the author's PeeTee Sportster design powered by a Saito 45 will do a clover leaf (where the model does four loops with a quarter roll on the downward part of each) without any trouble, while a similar sized sports model powered by a .25 cu.in. two-stroke lost so much height that the manoeuvre could not be completed when started at the same height as the four-stroke powered model. The PeeTee was kept at full throttle throughout the manoeuvre and so was the two-stroke powered model.

When the dust finally settles in the new "Turn around" pattern, the four-stroke will probably come out on top due to its ability to fly the model at a more constant speed without a lot of throttle work.

Chapter 10
The Way Ahead

It is always a dangerous thing to make predictions, in years to come others will draw attention to anything that has been shown to be completely wrong. However, it is always interesting to speculate on future developments.

The natural direction of progress is to seek more power and this trend will continue until four-strokes equal two-strokes. This is already happening in one or two cases and will eventually cause problems where contest rules allow .60 cu.in. two-strokes and 1.20 cu.in. four-strokes.

The search for more power may produce engines with more than the current two valves per cylinder and will possibly see overhead camshafts, even valves that are mechanically closed instead of relying on springs, these are called desmodromic valves. The rotary valve will also be a great contributor to more powerful engines.

It would seem possible that even turbo-chargers may be developed and sold as bolt on accessories and there may well be a constant speed propeller to make the best use of the power of the four-stroke, which will be cheaper than the current servo-controlled variable pitch propellers.

The attraction of the four-stroke with its quietness and economy will slowly be reduced by the increases in power output. There is a likelihood that side valve four-strokes will be developed, which will have all the advantages we now associate with the four-stroke but which will also be much shorter, making them very popular for scale models.

Every so often there arises a need for a new class of racing model because the previous "simple" racing has become dominated by the specialist and become too expensive and too fast for the average sports modeller to enjoy. It would not be unreasonable to expect the next "simple" racing class to be limited to models powered by .40 cu.in. four-strokes. This would limit speeds and noise and would probably give close, exciting racing at speeds that would allow pilots time to think and so be a more relaxing form of racing.

With regard to the capacity of four-strokes, they may get larger although the 60cc engines that are now on the horizon seem to be getting near to the maximum for current trends on large models in general use. There is the strong possiblity of a ⅕th scale 14 cylinder twin row Pratt & Whitney Wasp of 220cc capacity (14 cu.in.) being built on a limited scale.

It seems unlikely that many smaller engines than the HP VT 21 will be manufactured although the possibllity of a .15 cu.in. engine cannot be ruled out, this would most likely be a horizontal rotary valve, belt driven like the Webra range. We shall see.

Flight Test Reports

Reports on engines in magazines normally give details of brake horsepower and a series of r.p.m. figures against different sizes of propeller. These are excellent for statistical comparison of the various engines but the author has heard many modellers asking for flight testing and there can be no doubt that flight tests are of far more use to the average modeller. For example, the fact that a PAW 29 R/C diesel will just fly a seven foot span, seven pound "Powerhouse" will tell the modeller that the engine will be more than adequate for anything smaller. Mere r.p.m. and propellers will not give the same information.

The author has used almost every four-stroke engine under .60 cu.in. and some .60 cu.in. engines. Some of the models have had more than one engine fitted for testing purposes and in some cases the models have originally flown with two-stroke engines and some engines have been used in more than one model.

The test reports given in this section are not intended to show which is the perfect model size for any engine, they are intended to give a starting point from which the modeller can estimate the suitability of an engine/aircraft combination. Some reports show that the model was at the upper limits for the engine while others are at the opposite extreme.

These tests have a secondary value. They will allow the modeller to make more use of propeller/r.p.m. figures by allowing him to compare the figures for a tested engine against those for an engine not covered by the tests and so estimate how an alternative engine will fly a given model. Fuels, plugs, weather and even make of propeller will make a difference to performance figures but the starting point is there.

The technical information given covers most areas, however actual flight performance cannot be accurately measured and only an impression can be given. The aerobatics performed with most models will always give an indication of the amount of reserve power available, this is always useful information because the only real proof of an engine's usefulness is how it flies a model.

The 66in. span Super Scorpion is an ideal model for four-stroke power, the author's has an Enya 35-4C and is hardly ever used at full power.

Enya 35-4C

The Enya 35-4C is no longer listed but there are still some around. It was a very nice engine when properly handled, the main trouble was that 15% nitro fuel was recommended but the compression ratio was a little high for this fuel.

The engine used by the author was first installed in a Pilot kit Tiger Moth. The fuel used was 15% standard and a propeller from the lower end of the range was used. The model flew very well and the flight characteristics closely duplicated the full size aircraft, even to the extent that if too much down elevator was applied in a slow roll the roll stopped. This was the model that was mistaken for the full size as described in Chapter 1.

The Enya was next installed in a Super Scorpion, this is a 66in. span vintage model with a wing area of 779 sq.in. and a weight of 5lbs which gives a wing loading of 14.78 ounces per sq.ft. The engine was fitted with a Graupner 12 x 5 propeller and this caused severe detonation. An 0.008in. aluminium head gasket was fitted and the fuel was changed to 5% nitro with 20% oil. In this form the engine has given hours of service, flights of 40 minutes on a 6 ounce tank being normal, as most of the flight is at low throttle.

An interesting discovery was made with this model. The exhaust pipe was extended with silicone tubing to get the oil clear of the model. On one flight the model was coming in for a low, slow pass but was a bit too low so the throttle was opened up, but there was no power from the engine. After a few moment of very hairy flying between some trees the model was successfully landed and it was found that a hole had been blown throughout the silicone tubing close to the end of the exhaust pipe, opening the needle valve cured the fault at once as did replacing the tubing. This indicates that exhaust pipe length is worth experimenting with.

Mention has been made of fitting an aluminium gasket, this is not essential as the engine would have run perfectly on straight methanol/castor oil mixture which would also reduce the risk of corrosion.

Louise Gentry holding the author's ¼ scale Polish homebuilt, the 7lb 74in. model is adequately powered by an Enya 40-4C.

Enya 40-4C

The Enya 40-4C was fitted to a quarter scale Polish homebuilt aircraft called "Don Kichot" ("Don Quixote"). The aircraft features a pusher layout with the engine on top of the wing. The model has a wing area of 680 sq.in. and weighs 7lbs which gives a wing loading of 23.6 ounces per square foot. The wing is Clark Y section and is of a high aspect ratio (8:1) the fuselage is bulky but streamlined.

The engine was run on 15% nitro fuel and used a home made propeller which was 11¾ x 5 with wide blades. With this set up the model has more than enough power and is capable of loops, rolls, rolls off the top, stall turns and spins. Take offs from grass are quite easy even when the grass is 3in. long. Climb out is very rapid.

Flights with 5% nitromethane were also made and the model was still able to do the manoeuvres although there was no reserve of power and more speed had to be built up in a slight dive.

Other propellers were tested with a 15% nitro fuel but none of them gave as good a performance, including a similar propeller but with more pitch, about 11½ x 6 in this case.

There are one or two interesting points about this model, the propeller is very close to the trailing edge of the wing and cabin, as a result of this the noise was frightful, a very high pitched buzz which completely drowned all engine noise. The model showed very marked changes of pitch trim at different engine settings, in-flight photos showed quite noticeable changes of elevator settings at high and slow speed settings.

Pusher propellers are always more efficient than tractors and this must account for some of the performance but the model would have been adequately powered with a tractor propeller.

The author has plans of the same model to ⅓ scale by Podgorski, a top Polish scale modeller. This model is built mainly of ply wood and is powered by an O.S. FS60 and a Webra 40 two-stroke is shown on the plan.

The engine performed perfectly with superb throttling characteristics and has never cut in the air. The fuel tank is long and thin and faces forwards on the opposite side of the pylon from the engine, no fuel feed problems have been encountered.

ENYA

Enya 46-4C

The Enya 46-4C is a relatively new engine, it is very compact and closely follows the Enya design pattern. Unlike the 35-4C and 40-4C it features enclosed rocker arms and comes complete with a silencer.

The engine was fitted to the author's Druine Turbulent (see Saito FA-40 test for details of this model). The first flight was made with a Master 11 x 7½in. propeller on 15% standard fuel and performance was not appreciably better than with the Saito fitted. A change was then made to a Graupner 12 x 5in. propeller and the optional head gasket provided with the engine was fitted. The engine was transformed and the Turbulent performed more like a Spitfire. All aerobatics could be started from level flight while the engine never missed a beat regardless of attitude.

The noise level was very low at full throttle but when the throttle was cut back to half power, all that could be heard was a sort of rustling noise from the model which was about 100 yards away.

None of the smaller Enya engines have any provision for pressurising the fuel tank from the exhaust and this has never caused any problems.

The Enya 46-4C is a perfect engine for powering a scale model of any homebuilt aircraft which is fitted with a Volkswagen engine, if the model is built between ⅕th and ¼ scale, the Enya will be a very close match to the exposed VW engine.

The first really small four-stroke was the HP VT-21, which has proved its value in small, purpose built models.

HP VT 21

The HP VT 21 is the smallest four-stroke made at the time of writing. 3.5cc capacity and weighing almost 12 ounces, it features a rotary valve in the head driven by gears from the crank shaft via a vertical shaft and a second set of gears in the head.

The lubrication system is unusual in that the silencer pressure is fed to the cylinder head from where it drains down to the crankcase and out of a nipple on the crankshaft housing which is connected to the tank. Under certain circumstances this can lead to excess pressure in the tank and the manufacturers now recommend a tee piece in the line from the silencer to the head. The tank is pressurised from this tee piece and the nipple on the crankshaft housing is vented to atmosphere.

The engine needs high nitro four-stroke fuel, 15% nitro being needed. For the flight test 5% nitro four-stroke fuel mixed in equal amounts with 25% nitro glow fuel gave a slightly higher oil content.

The engine also prefers smaller propellers and best results on the test were with a Master propeller 9 x 4in.

The model was a high wing cabin model with 450 sq.in. of wing area and weighing 4lbs 4oz. giving 21¾ ounces per sq.ft.

The model flew quite well and was capable of loops if some speed was built up first, it was also capable of rolls and flick rolls and would continue climbing when the engine was well throttled back although the VT 21 will not throttle down to very low r.p.m.

While the test model flew it was felt that a model with a lower wing loading would have been much better. The engine is remarkably quiet even by four-stroke standards and a close low pass sounded more like a big rubber powered model with geared motors. In fact it is suspected that most of the noise is gear noise with some propeller noise.

Considering the small size of the engine and the friction of the gears and rotary valve which must absorb a considerable amount of the power it is a good performer and would be ideal for small field flying near to houses.

HP VT 49

This engine is the same design as the VT 21, however the silencer is attached to the end of a normal four-stroke exhaust pipe and is quite large, it is also very effective. The same system of lubrication is used but presumably the modification suggested at the end of the VT 21 test report would be a good idea.

The engine has been flown in a low wing aerobatic sports model which weighs 5lb 10oz and has a wing area of 594 sq.in. giving a wing loading of 21.8 oz per sq.ft.

The model had been flown previously with a K&B 40 and an MVVS 40 schnuerle port engine, with these engines the performance was very good with all normal aerobatics possible. Fitting the HP increased the weight by some 10 ounces, partly due to the need to add lead to the tail to counter the extra weight of the HP engine. With the HP a 12 x 6 Kavan propeller was used.

The take off seemed to be slightly longer with the HP but once in the air there was no noticeable difference in performance when compared to the two-stroke engines. However, the sound level was very much lower and fuel consumption was lower.

The silencer is held onto the exhaust pipe by a gland nut and ring, this must be very firmly tightened and should be tightened again when the engine is hot. The silencer did fall off in flight and there was a slight increase in sound level, fortunately the silencer was not lost as the pressure line held it until the model could be landed.

The engine does in fact weigh 21½oz even though the instructions state 22oz. This is still heavy for an engine of this size and it would be best suited to short nosed scale models or the extra weight taken into consideration when designing a model for the engine, alternatively the radio equipment could be moved further back in the fuselage.

The British Laser 61, one of the most powerful .60 sized four-strokes and highly competitive in price. This engine is used as the basis for the Laser 1.20 cu.in. 90° V twin.

Laser 61

The Laser 61 is a British engine, it is machined from the solid throughout and features a wedge shaped combustion chamber. When the engine was tested on the bench it equalled the power of the Merco 61 two-stroke before it was completely run in. On propellers over 13in. diameter it exceeded the Merco 61's r.p.m. even though the Merco was running on 5% nitro fuel while the Laser was running on straight methanol/castor mix.

Fuel consumption was very similar to the Merco while sound levels were only slightly lower.

The Laser was installed in a Multi-plex Big Lift, an 88in. span high wing cabin model. The wing area is 1,093 sq.in. and the weight is 10lbs giving a wing loading of 21 ounces per sq.ft. The model had previously been flown with a Merco 61. Propeller used on the Laser is a 13 x 5in. wood.

Performance was outstanding, the model would climb at about 45° if the throttle was opened after a gentle descent. The model could be flown down a fairly steep hill and then either full throttle would be signalled and the model would present a plan view as it climbed out or the model could be turned at the bottom of the hill and made to climb back up the slope. Both the descent and ascent could be made at a constant two feet above the ground. Bearing in mind that the Laser is always run on straight methanol/castor fuel this is proof of truly remarkable throttle response.

The Laser carburettor extends straight out from the cylinder head and so must be well above the fuel tank when mounted upright, this does not affect the engine which continues to run perfectly from a full tank to an empty one.

The author's 72in. span Sig Piper Cub is almost overpowered by the O.S. FS 40. The engine is inverted and enclosed rockers are commended. The engine could be side mounted if one with exposed rockers was used.

O.S. FS-40

The O.S. FS-40 has been fitted in two models, the first model was the Sig kit of the Piper J-3 Cub which is 72in. span and very light, the wing area and weight are unknown as the model has since been sold.

The Cub was flown using 5% standard glow fuel and a Master 11 x 7½ propeller. With this set up it was very nice, more than enough power, capable of looping from level flight and very difficult to get down with any power on at all. On a 6 ounce tank ½ hour and ¾ hour flights were commonplace. (I fly with a couple of friends and we are all on different frequencies so there is no problem with long flights.)

The O.S. FS-40 was next installed in a semi-scale cropduster, this model, the Agro-Cat, had a wingspan of 55in. and an area of 600 sq.in. and weight of 5lb 6oz. which gives a wing loading of 20.5oz per sq.ft. Section is flat bottomed, roughly Clark Y, the model is fitted with slotted ailerons and slotted flaps and has a dust hopper, it is flown on 5% nitro four-stroke fuel and a Kavan 11 x 6 prop.

The model has a really good performance, all normal aerobatics are possible although vertical manoeuvres are limited to stall turns. The model can be flown at very low speeds and yet still accelerate away as soon as the throttle is opened, the very good throttle control allows this without fear of cutting at the wrong moment.

The most interesting part of this test is that the model can be loaded with over 1lb of Plaster of Paris for dusting and this increases the wing loading to around 24.5oz per sq.ft., a 20% increase. At this weight the model can still be hand launched (some sites call for this) and will perform well but the extra weight is noticeable, climb out is reduced and the model is less lively but still capable of rolls and loops althogh very little aerobatting has been done in the loaded state.

As the dust is dropped the change is obvious as the model becomes more responsive to the controls. Fully loaded take-offs are not so easy on grass but landings are only a little faster.

The first start of a flying session takes a few moments but after that starts are very quick.

The exhaust pipe on this engine has a tendency to crack round the flange, spares are cheap and it would be good policy to keep one on hand.

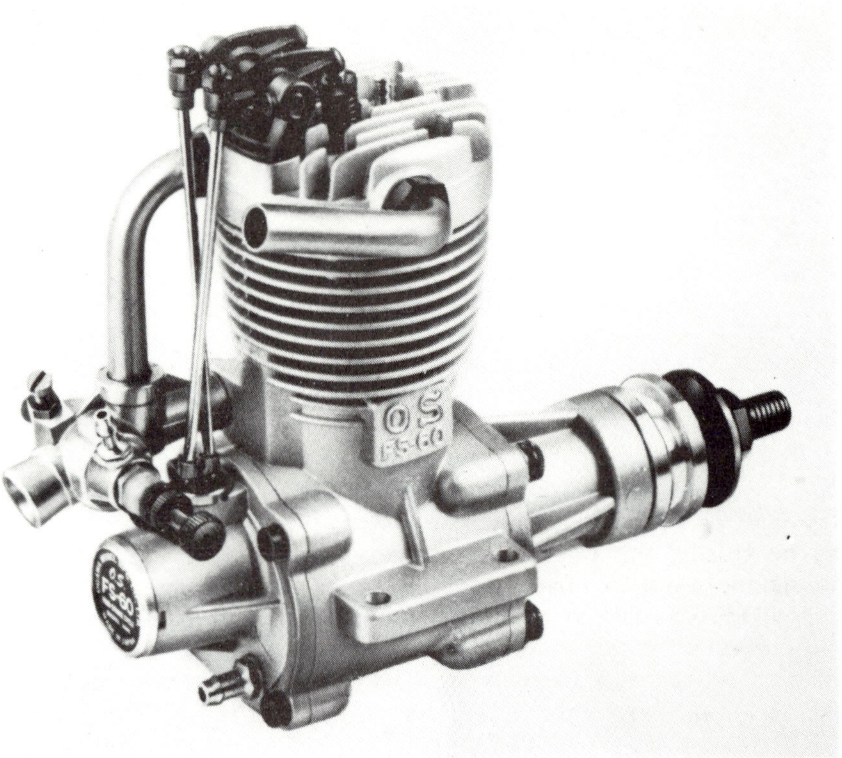

The author's current camera plane, fitted with the OS FS60.

O.S. FS-60

The O.S. FS-60 is the engine that really introduced four-strokes to the world. True, it was actually preceded by the Kalt 45 but Kalts are comparatively rare even now.

The O.S. was first installed in a Bi-Stormer 60 which it flew well but the model didn't last long due to pilot error. The next model was the Pilot Kit Bellanca Decathlon which was about 66in. span and weighed in the region of 7lbs. In this model the O.S. was excellent and could pull the model through most aerobatics although vertical manoeuvres were not really possible. The engine was run on standard 5% glowfuel and used a 12 x 6 wood propeller, endurance was around 25 minutes at full throttle on an 8 ounce tank. This combination was nearly perfect although a lighter model would have improved things.

The FS-60 was next fitted to a camera plane. This model has a fuselage about 6 x 7in. in cross section and has a wingspan of 72in. Area is 864 sq.in. and weight is 144 ounces giving a wing loading of 24 ounces per sq.ft. With fuel and propeller as for the Decathlon, performance was very good. An indication of the reserve power is the fact that if the split flaps were deployed at full throttle the model would instantly do a loop. The engine was replaced in the camera plane with a Merco 61 mainly because the lower vibration frequency of the four-stroke caused the camera to vibrate, the Merco also gave more power for rough field take-offs.

The O.S. is now in New Zealand flying a Super Buccaneer and giving 15 minute flights on a tank of less than 4 ounces. FS-60s are the most common power unit for Keil Kraft Falcons, a large 7ft. span vintage model which tends to be heavier than the average, although wing loading will be quite low.

FA30
MADE IN JAPAN

Saito FA-30

The Saito FA-30 tested was one of the first in this country as it was bought from an American shop before any importer had taken on marketing the engine here. This early Saito FA-30 was different to the current engine in several ways, the rocker arms were of the tall pattern and the carburettor plugged directly into the cylinder head, unlike the current engine which has a manifold which brings the carb into the same location as the 40 and 45. Because of the high location of the carb a restrictor was supplied which fitted into the throttle barrel and reduced the bore to a mere 3mm, this was to improve fuel draw.

The engine was fitted to a Super 60 with four function radio gear. The model weighed 5lbs and had previously been flown with a Fox 29. The Saito did not of course equal the power of the Fox but it flew the model well and had enough power to throw it around with loops and rolls, etc.

Fuel was standard 5% nitro glow fuel and the prop normally used was 10 x 6. The engine always started easily.

The engine was later converted by buying a Saito FA-40 manifold and exhaust pipe with pressure tapping and was used by a friend in his Junior 60 vintage model. Apart from take off, the engine was never run at full power in this model the rate of climb being spectacular and not in keeping with the vintage atmosphere.

It is interesting to note that this engine was bought in the very early days of four-strokes and long before the problem of corrosion was known. It was frequently flown and then stored for quite long periods with no oil being injected into the crankcase after flying. Before the engine was passed on to my friend it was inspected for corrsion and apart from staining of the crankshaft and a little pitting on the outside of the rear ball race there was none to speak of, possibly this was due to always using castor oil based fuel.

The current engine with its smaller rocker arms and the low set carb should be even more powerful.

The author's Ryan B-5 Brougham uses a Saito 40, note how well it blends into the dummy radial engine.

Saito FA-40

This particular engine is the early version with exposed rocker arms, the later version may possibly be a little more powerful.

The Saito FA-40 has been flown in two models, the first model was a scale Ryan B-5 Brougham which is virtually the same as the Ryan NYP Spirit of St Louis. The model was 63in. wingspan and had about 567 sq.in. of area, the weight was about 6lbs which gave a wing loading of 24 oz. per sq.ft. The engine was fitted with a Kavan 11 x 6 propeller and used standard 5% glowfuel.

The Ryan was adequately powered for scale flight, it would take off from longish grass and was fast in flight but not aerobatic. The Clark Y wing section provided lift at the high wing loading and the model would maintain altitutde on about half throttle.

The engine was then installed in a 2/9ths scale Turbulent, this model has a wingspan of 58in. and 600 sq.in. of area. Weight is 5lbs 8oz which give a wing loading of 21 oz per sq.ft., the section is a scale semi-symmetrical one. Originally the model was flown on standard 5% flow fuel and the Kavan 11 x 6 propeller and performance was good with most normal aerobatics possible.

Later the model was flown on 5% four-stroke fuel and this transformed the Turbulent. Power was noticeably increased and the idle was superb, prolonged descents with the engine ticking over could be followed by a rapid climb out and all aerobatics became that much easier. The model also stayed very clean. A four ounce fuel tank would give 20 minute flights and still leave some fuel in the tank.

The model is quite light and this has paid off when on one occasion it flew into some scrap farm machinery without any serious damage, a loose tailplane which was fixed with Cyano in a few minutes and, later, when it clobbered a bulldozer cab and suffered no damage.

The model has now been re-engined for testing other engines, see Enya 46-4C test.

The author's Pee Tee Sportster is aerobatic on the Saito 45 with good low speed handling.

Saito FA-45

The Saito FA-45 has been flown in one model only, the PeeTee Sportster. This model weighs 5lbs 4oz and has a wing area of 540 sq.in. which gives a wing loading of 22.4oz. per sq.ft. The wing section is semi-symmetrical.

The engine is run on standard 5% glow fuel and an 11 x 7½ propeller. The use of 10 nitro four-stroke fuel does not seem to make any real difference to this engine, unlike the Saito FA-40.

The model is reasonably aerobatic, loops, rolls and inverted being easy without any need to build up speed in a dive before doing a loop. Vertical performance is limited although upwards half rolls are possible. The model does not build up very much extra speed in a dive and the clover leaf (four loops with a quarter roll on the downward side) is quite easy even at full throttle all the way.

The model will take off from quite long grass but can also be hand launched very easily.

The propeller mentioned is the one recommended in the instructions and the one used is a Master airscrew. A Graupner 11 x 7½ with wide blades has been tried but did not make any great improvement. It is possible that a finer pitch propeller with wide blades might increase the climb but the model performs quite satisfactorily as it is.

Fuel consumption is about 6 ounces in 20 minutes at full throttle which is about right compared to other engines of this size.

The engine is fitted with a choke and this is very effective.

The 7ft. span 10 lb Multiplex Big Lift has been flown with a Merco 61, it flies as well or better with the Laser 61 and has also been used to test fly the Saito FA 90T.

Saito FA-90T

This flat twin is a 15cc engine which is remarkably light at about 26 ounces. The engine tested was the last Saito 90 available before the improved version arrived in the country.

The engine was fitted to a model and ground runs made, as the recommended 15 x 4 prop was not available a 14 x 6 was used and a couple of tankfulls of standard 5% glow fuel run through it.

Like most four-strokes it started first flick out of the box and ran well from the start. The engine has two carburettors in one body and setting them is a little tricky. This is not helped by the fact that the right exhaust pipe is slightly closed at the end to provide pressure for the fuel tank while the other exhaust is open, this gives a different exhaust note to each cylinder. Another factor which it must be said is not helpful is the instruction leaflet which is in Japanese English. A supplementary leaflet is even more confusing but is amusing to try and read. Hopefully the next Saito twin will have better instructions. Once the instructions have been worked out setting the carbs is not too difficult, but it is felt that onboard nicads switched in at low throttle to heat the plugs would be a good idea.

One interesting characteristic noticed was that when one side was adjusted until that cylinder stopped firing, reversing of the adjustment would often start that cylinder firing again without connecting the battery to the plug.

The model used in the test was the Big Lift (see Laser 61 test). The Saito flew this in about the same way as the Laser. It was necessary to throttle back a long way to stop the model climbing and opening up to full power after a low flypast would result in a 45° climb out. Acceleration on take off was not quite as rapid but with the correct propeller would probably be as good or better, also at the time of writing the engine is still relatively new and has not been set for maximum performance. In this state the engine is more than adequate to fly a 7 foot span 10lb model so it can safely be assumed that larger models will be well within its capabilities when fully run in.

The Webra 40 4-T showing drive belt cover and carb location. The larger Webra four-strokes have the carb mounted on a manifold to lower them.

Webra 40 4-T

This engine features a rotary valve which is driven by toothed belt from the crankshaft. Like most rotary valved engines the Webra likes smaller propellers.

The engine was fitted to the Super Scorpion described in the Enya 35-4C test which it flew with about the same apparent ease even though it was still being run in at the time.

The high location of the carb on the cylinder does mean that the muffler pressure has to be used and a high tank location is preferred. If the engine is mounted sidewinder fashion it would be best if the carb was on top which would mean that the cylinder would be on the left side of the model. This is no problem as the right side mounting of engines is due to tradition from control line models and the fact that most two-strokes have the exhaust on the right and by mounting them with the cylinder on the right the silencer points downwards and so is less noticeable and keeps the model cleaner. The Webra exhaust pipe can be swung through 360° and is mounted at the rear of the cylinder so this is no longer a problem.

An unusually large spanner is needed to tighten the lock nut for the exhaust pipe (17/32 AF).

In flight the engine showed superb throttle control and response with excellent idle. Plug used was a standard Taylor with 5% standard glow fuel. The engine was very quiet and would seem to be an excellent choice for vintage models and scale models of the slower flying prototypes.

APPENDIX
Notes on Table of Four-Stroke Engines

The date for this table has been taken from the engine instructions or manufacturer's leaflets and some features may vary due to changes in design etc. e.g. the HP VT engines actually weigh less in the case of the VT 49 and more in the case of the VT 21.

R.P.M. is given as the maximum recommended depending on propeller. Idle r.p.m. has not been given as this will be fairly standard at around 2500 r.p.m. although lower figures may be obtained at the cost of reliable pick up from idle or by arranging for a battery to heat the plugs at low r.p.m.

An asterisk* by a propeller indicates that this is the only size given but other sizes could be used, the rule being to decrease pitch when increasing diameter and increase pitch when reducing the diameter. It is worth testing a series of propellers on any given model to find the best for that model/engine combination.

A dagger† by an engine indicates that it is included in the flight test section of the book.

Some of the engines listed are not normally available in this country but may be obtained through contacts abroad. Some engines are no longer made but are included as they may still be available as second hand engines.

From the way that engines are appearing on the market, it is obvious that this list will soon become outdated, therefore space has been left at the end of the table to add these as details are published in the model press.

It is interesting to note that there are no American four-strokes apart from the Technopower engines which were originally made in Ireland. The ⅕th scale Pratt & Whitney twin row Wasp projected by William M. Hawke in the USA has not been included as it is a very limited run and at the time of writing is not 100% certain to be produced.

Table of Four-Stroke Engines

Name	*Capacity*	*WT*	*RPM Range*	*Prop Sizes*	*Remarks*
Condor	.91 cu.in.	34 oz	6–11000	14x6–7 15x8	These engines have an integral fuel pump
Condor	1.20 cu.in.	32 oz	6–11000	18x5	
Damo	18cc	24½ oz	7–10000	14x6 to 18x5	Needs no oil although some is permissible
Ehmo	10cc	530 gr	9000	No data	Not imported
† Enya	.35 cu.in.	345 gr	12000	10x6 to 12x4	Discontinued
† Enya	.40 cu.in.	365 gr	12000	10x6 to 12x4	
† Enya	.46 cu.in.	365 gr	13000	10x6 to 13x5	
Enya	.60 cu.in.	595 gr	7–11000	11x8 to 16x4	
Enya	.90 cu.in.	795 gr	7–11000	11.5x7 to 16x6	
Enya	1.20 cu.in.	800 gr	7–11000	11.5x7 to 16x6	
† H.P.	.21 cu.in.	300 gr	Up to 15000	7x6 to 9x5	Rotary valve
† H.P.	.49 cu.in.	640 gr	Up to 13000	10x7 to 14x4	
Jupiter	18.5cc	1200 gr	9000	18x6	O.H.C.
Jupiter	37cc	1800 gr	7300	18x8	Flat twin using parts of 18.5 cc engine. Not imported.
Kalt	.45 cu.in.				Not generally available.
Kavan	50cc	2,450 gr	8000	18x12 to 20x10	Wet sump with oil pump. Copy of full size Continental engine.
Laser	.60 cu.in.	24 oz	10000	12x6 to 14x7	
Laser	.75 cu.in.	24 oz	10800	12x6 to 14x7	
Laser	.90 cu.in.	28 oz	11400	12x6 to 14x7	
Laser	1.20	34 oz	12500	12x6 to 15x8	V twin
Magnum	.90 cu.in.				Reverse push rods for reverse rotation
Magnum	1.20 cu.in.	No data received from			V twin
Magnum	2.7 cu.in.	manufacturer			3 cylinder radial
† O.S.	.40 cu.in.	340 gr	10000	10.5x6 to 12x5	
† O.S.	.60 cu.in.	560 gr	10000	12x6 to 13x5½	Obsolete
O.S.	.61 cu.in.	540 gr	11000	11x7 to 14x6	
O.S.	.80 cu.in.	605 gr	11000	11x7 to 13x5	
O.S.	.90 cu.in.	645 gr	11000	11x7 to 14x5	
O.S.	1.20 cu.in.	765	11000	14x8 to 18x6	
O.S.	1.20 cu.in.	980 gr	9000	16x6 to 18x6	Gemini twin
O.S.	1.60 cu.in.	1,100 gr	10000	15x8 to 20x6	Gemini 160, new design, not a bored 120

† Saito	.30 cu.in.	320 gr	10000	10x4 to 11x4	ABC engine exposed rockers
† Saito	.40 cu.in.	340 gr	10000	11x4 to 12x4	AAC engine rockers enclosed on later model
† Saito	.45 cu.in.	380 gr	10000	11x7½, 12x5	
† Saito	.90 cu.in.	740 gr	9000	15x4*	Flat twin using Saito 45 parts. Single throw crank.
Saito	1.20 cu.in.	920 gr	10000	15x6*	
Saito	2.70 cu.in.	2,200 gr	8000	20x8*	
Technopower	1.35 cu.in.	30 oz	9000	14x6 to 16x8	3 cylinder radial
Technopower	1.39 cu.in.	26 oz	9000	14x6*	5 cylinder radial spark or glow
Technopower	1.35 cu.in.	31 oz	9000	14x6*	7 cylinder radial
Technopower	3.6 cu.in.	4½ lbs	9000	18x8 to 24x6	9 cylinder radial
† Webra	.40 cu.in.	380 gr	11000	10x4 to 11x7½	Belt drive rotary
Webra	.60 cu.in.	600 gr	Not	12x8 to 13x6	valves on all
Webra	.80 cu.in.	640 gr	known	13x8 to 14x6	Webra 4 strokes

Notes to Glossary

The brief glossary is intended for those who may be new to modelling or new to four-stroke engines.

Most terms are explained as they occur in the text. However, there are some which are not used in the text but do appear in engine instructions and some articles about engines, also one or two which are used by American modellers instead of the terms we use.

No attempt has been made to make this a complete glossary of all model engine terms because it would become too complex if every basic item was described.

Glossary

AAC. Used to describe an engine which has an *A*luminiumum piston running in an *A*luminium cylinder which has been *C*hrome plated. This arrangement gives better cooling, less likelihood of seizure and makes the engine lighter. Running in should be at a fast but rich setting to allow the engine to reach running temperature quickly. Some AAC engines are very tight when new, even to the extent that they literally squeak at the top of the stroke.

ABC. Similar to AAC but using a *B*rass cylinder which has been *C*hrome plated. Most of the remarks regarding AAC apply except the weight which will be roughly the same as a normal engine.

Beam mounting. *See* **Mounting.**

Cam. An eccentric lobe which is used to lift the valve through a train of rods and levers.

Cam follower. A piece of steel which slides in a bearing in the timing chest to provide a large bearing surface on which the cam can push.

Cam shaft. A shaft driven at half the engine speed and which carries the cams, the cams may be an integral part of the shaft or may be separate but firmly attached to it.

Cuban Eight. A simple aerobatic manoeuvre where the model performs most of a loop but as it reaches the inverted 45° angle is rolled until it is upright, and the same sequence is carried out again forming the shape of a Number 8 lying on its side. This manoeuvre can be flown continuously by most models and is an excellent way of running in an engine in the air as it loads the engine lightly and then unloads it thus giving the engine some work to do without allowing it to get too hot.

Cycle, two, four. The American term for two or four-stroke engines. The Japanese normally say 'four-stroke cycle' which is the correct terminology.

Desmodromic Valves. *See* **Valves.**

Flat Twin, four, six. A "flat" engine is a multi-cylinder engine with the cylinders on opposite sides of the crankshaft. A flat twin would have one each side while a flat six would have three on each side of the shaft. They are usually mounted horizontally, hence the "flat". The correct term is horizontally opposed.

Hydraulic lock. This occurs when excess fuel has entered the cylinder and the piston cannot reach the top of the stroke. It is vital that no attempt be made to turn the engine over as damage will result. The lock can be cleared by turning the propeller backwards and forwards over the area of free travel until the excess fuel is ejected through the exhaust ports. If the engine is upright it may be necessary to turn the model over until the exhaust pipe is pointing downwards.

In Line. A multi-cylinder engine where the cylinders are all arranged one behind the other.

Lean Mixture. *See* **Mixture.**

Manifold. Within modelling, the pipe connecting the carburettor to the cylinder head, may also refer to a pipe joining exhausts to a silencer.

Mixture, rich, lean, weak. Mixture refers to the fuel-air mixture. A rich mixture is one with too much fuel while a lean or weak mixture is one with too little. The rich mixture is revealed by large amounts of smoke and even raw fuel being ejected from the exhaust. A lean mixture will have very little smoke or oil and detonation may set in (see Chapter 5). An engine should always be run slightly rich to prevent overheating and detonation and to allow for any tendency to lean out as the fuel level drops in the tank.

Mounting, beam, radial. Beam mounting is where two arms extend forward from the front bulkhead or firewall, the engine is secured by bolts through lugs cast onto the crankcase. Radial mounting is where the engine has a flange or lugs and is bolted direct to the bulkhead. Various types of radial mounts are available which in effect convert a beam mount engine to a radial mount type. There are no conversions for radially mounted engines to convert them to beam mount.

Nitromethane. An additive for fuel which releases oxygen when burnt and so gives increased power. In small amounts it also improves the slow running on many engines. Normally 5, 10 or 15% nitro is used in four-strokes while a few do not need any. Nitromethane is expensive and so engines that will run well on smaller quantities of nitro will be more economical. As the amount of nitro is increased more fuel will be used as the needle valve has to be opened further.

Opposed twin. *See* **Flat twin.**

Pitch. Propellers are described by two numbers, eg. 10x6. The first number is the diameter and the second number is the pitch. Pitch refers to the amount of angle of the blade and is the theoretical distance that the propeller would travel if it was screwing itself through a solid substance. It has always been assumed that one should allow for 10% "slip" when calculating theoretical speeds from the pitch/r.p.m. combination. However, modellers using audio tachometers which give r.p.m. reading from the engine frequency and accurate timing over a measured distance have found that speeds have exceeded the maximum possible when only the pitch and r.p.m. are calculated which would indicate that the lift from the airfoil section of the blade plays a very important role in thrust development.

Poppet Valve. *See* **Valves.**

Pushrod. The rod that transfers the motion from the cam follower to the rocker arm.

Radial engines. Multi cylinder engines where the cylinders are arranged like the spokes of a wheel. Advantages are: lighter due to smaller crankcase and short crankshaft, better cooling of all cylinders. Disadvantages: large frontal area, more complex system of cams and cam drives.

Radial Mount. *See* **Mounting.**

Rich Mixture. *See* **Mixture.**

Rocker arm. A lever mounted on the cylinder head and pivoted near its centre which transfers the motion from the pushrod to the valve. Normally has the tappet adjuster on one end.

Rotary Valve. *See* **Valve.**

Side Valve. *See* **Valve.**

Single throw crankshaft. *See* **Throw.**

Tappet Clearance. The gap between the end of the rocker arm and the valve stem. This gap allows for expansion of various parts of the engine and ensures that the valve will close fully. Must be checked from time to time and re-set if necessary.

Throw, single, double. Twin cylinder engines may have the connecting rods on one crank pin in which case they are known as single throw, or two crankpins in which case they are double throw shafts. A flat twin may be either, an inline engine must be double throw.

Timing. Normally applied to valves but also applies to the timing of the spark on spark ignition engines. Normally measured in degrees of crankshaft revolution before or after the piston reches the top of the cylinder, or Top dead centre (TDC).

Timing Chest. The chamber or compartment where the cams, cam gears and cam followers are located.

Valve. The part that opens and closes allowing the mixture to enter the cylinder and the exhaust to escape.

Desmodromic. A valve that is mechanically closed rather than relying on a spring. Normally applied to poppet valves. Not in use on model engines yet.

Needle. The method of controlling the flow of fuel to the carburettor being a tapered needle with a screw thread which screws in to reduce fuel flow. There is always a needle valve for high speed running and some engines have a second one to control fuel flow at the slow speed setting of the throttle.

Overhead. Valves fitted in the cylinder head, normally poppet valves. This allows a smaller combustion chamber and more efficient combustion chamber shape.

Poppet. Mushroom shaped valve which seals the end of the inlet or exhaust port and which is lifted from its seat by the action of the cam via the cam follower, pushrod and rocker arm. The poppet valve can limit the top speed of the engine due to the fact that the spring may not be able to close it fast enough and a condition may be reached where the valve never fully closes with resultant loss of efficiency, this is known as valve float. The piston may hit the valve under some circumstances.

Rotary. A cylindrical or disc valve which rotates, ports in the valve uncovers the inlet port and exhaust port in turn and, in some engines also uncovers the glowplug. Rotary valves may be driven by gears or belts, the latter being the simplest of all methods of driving the valves.

Side. Poppet valves fitted beside the cylinder and having part of the combustion chamber extending over them. Side valves do not need rocker arms, there is no risk of them hitting the piston and the engine need be no taller than the average two-stroke but they do not allow as efficient a shape for the combustion chamber.

Timing. The moment the valves open, close and the length of time that they are open. This is normally measured in degrees of crankshaft rotation from top or bottom dead centre, top and bottom dead centre being the position of the piston in the cylinder when the crankpin is at its highest or lowest position. Measurements are before or after TDC or BDC and are written e.g. 15° BTDC or BBDC etc.

Vee Twin. A twin cylinder engine where the cylinders are arranged in a V-shape, the angle may vary but 90° is common. A single throw crankshaft is used.

Wankel engine. A unique engine design which does not use pistons but has a roughly triangular rotor in a roughly 8 shaped chamber. The rotor drives the crankshaft through gearing. Several amateur builders have made Wankel engines but the only commercially made model Wankel engine is the O.S. .30 cu.in. engine originally developed by Graupner.

Weak Mixture. *See* **Mixture.**

Wing loading. One of the most important figures in model design and found by dividing the model's weight by the wing area. Optimum wing loading for models powered by four-strokes of less than .60 cu.in. is 22 ounces per square foot or less.

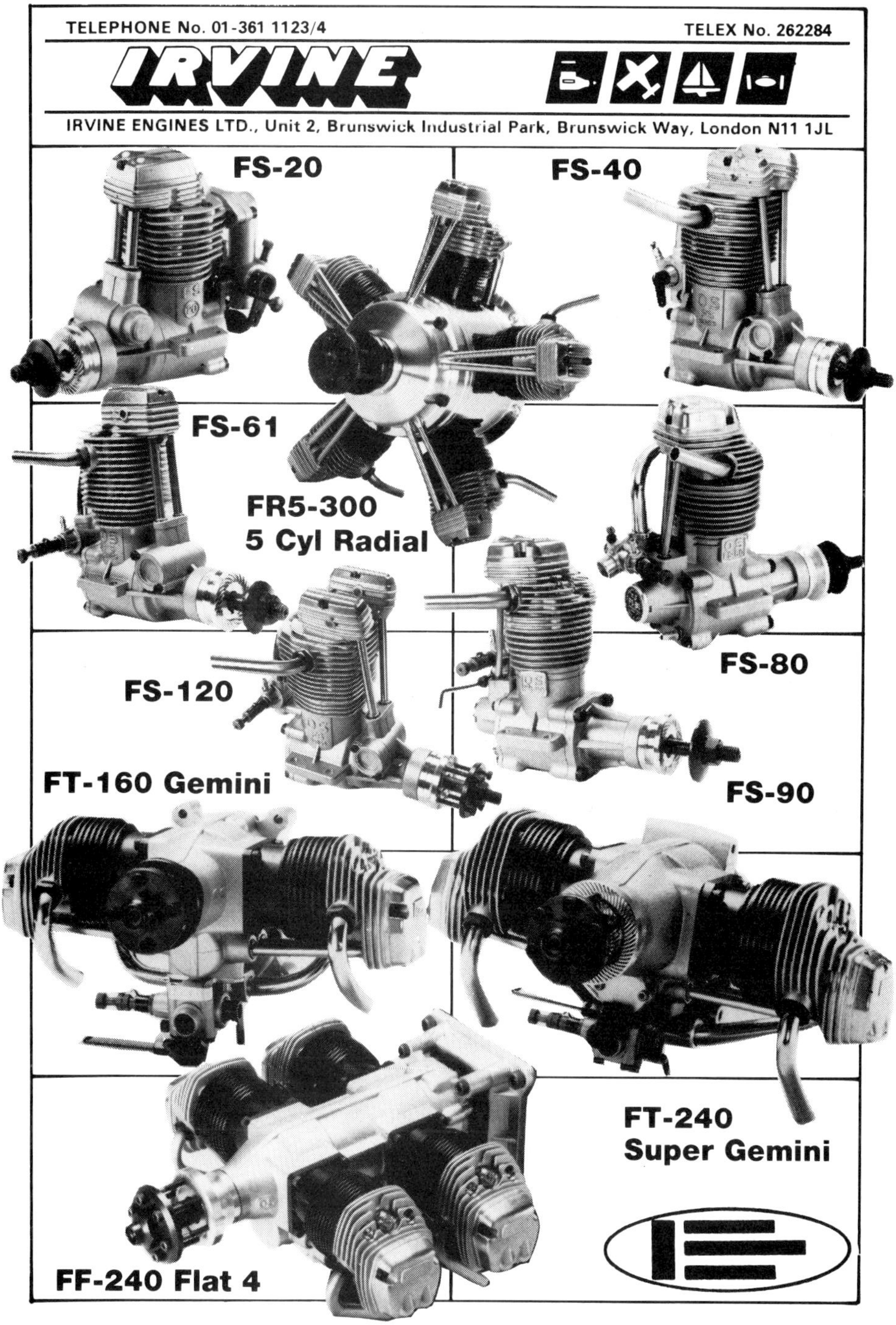
TELEPHONE No. 01-361 1123/4
TELEX No. 262284
IRVINE
IRVINE ENGINES LTD., Unit 2, Brunswick Industrial Park, Brunswick Way, London N11 1JL
FS-20
FS-40
FS-61
FR5-300
5 Cyl Radial
FS-80
FS-120
FS-90
FT-160 Gemini
FT-240
Super Gemini
FF-240 Flat 4

THE BRILLIANCE OF SAITO
SAITO
SAITO
FA-90T
Bore 22.4 mm x 2 Stroke 19 mm x 2 Displacement .45 cu ins x 2/ 7.5cc x 2 Weight approx. 26.10 oz (740 grams) Normal RPM 9,000 (15 x 5)
FA-30
Bore 19.3mm Stroke 17mm Displacement .30 cu ins/5cc Weight approx. 11.28 oz (320 grams. Normal RPM 11,000 (10x4)
FA-40
Bore 21 mm Stroke 19mm Displacement .40 cu ins/6.5cc Weight approx. 13.75 oz (390 grams) Normal RPM 10,000 (12 x 4)
FA-40W
Bore 21 mm Stroke 19 mm Displacement .40 cu ins/6.5cc Weight approx. 13.75 oz (390 grams) Normal RPM 10,000
SAITO
FA-30W
Bore 19.3mm Stroke 17mm Displacement .30 cu ins/5cc Weight approx. 11.28 oz (320 grams) Normal RPM 11,000
FA-120
Bore 32mm Stroke 24.8mm Displacement 1.20 cu ins/ 20cc Weight approx. 32.45 oz (920 grams) RPM 10,000 (18 x 6)
FA-45
Bore 22.4 mm Stroke 19mm Displacement .45 cu ins/ 7.5cc. Weight 13.4 oz (380 grams) RPM 10,000 (14 x 4)
For those who appreciate the finer points of engineering
SAITO .45 £98·95
New Saito 65 £139·00
'AAC' aluminium piston in a chrome plated aluminium sleeve.
Hemispherical combustion chamber for extra power.
Choke valve for easy starting.
High tension steel for extra strength.
Additional needle valve for reliable tickover and low RPM adjustment.
All this adds up to engines with high power to weight ratios that last, run quietly, have low vibration levels, are economic on fuel and start easily.
Machined rocker arms pivoting on stainless steel shafts.
Large valves for improved breathing.
Twin Ballraces.
Superb castings machined to fine tolerances with special gauges for a perfect machined fit.
When thinking FOUR STROKES – think SAITO because when it comes to internal combustion engines that's all that SAITO think about.
All these magnificently engineered four stroke engines are supplied with a choke valve, extension lever for choke valve, needle valve extension bar, exhaust pipe, feeler gauge and comprehensive tool kit.
For further information send an S.A.E. to: MacGregor Industries Limited, Canal Estate, Langley, Berkshire. Telephone: Slough 42251/2/3.
MacGregor